RAIN FROM HEAVEN

RAIN FROM HEAVEN

Revival in Scripture and History

by
Arthur Wallis

HODDER AND STOUGHTON
AND CHRISTIAN LITERATURE CRUSADE

British Library Cataloguing in Publication Data
Wallis, Arthur

  1. Revivals
  I. Title
  269'.2   BV3790

Rain from Heaven. Revival in Scripture and History
ISBN 0 340 23807 0

INTRODUCTION - OLD YET NEW

This book is old yet new. It is old because in essence it is a book published over twenty years ago under the title, *In the Day of Thy Power – The Scriptural Principles of Revival* (Christian Literature Crusade, 1956). God used it to stir up desire and faith for the outpouring of the Spirit in our day. I met ministers who told me that they had read it through two or three times. Others said that they were using it for group study in their ministers' fraternal or revival prayer group.

In the Day of Thy Power was a hardback which eventually went into four editions. When the publishers approached me a few years ago about re-issuing it as a paperback, I discouraged them from doing so. I felt that it had the characteristic faults of a first book. It was too long and too heavy for the average reader. Even more important, it needed to be brought up-to-date in the light of all that had transpired since it was first issued, not only in the church but in the author's heart! I promised to revise, if not to re-write it. At long last the promise has been fulfilled. It has proved to be a re-writing rather than merely a revision; hence the new title.

Those who possess a copy of the old book will find that among a number of omissions are some of the chapters on prayer. This is not because I now disagree with what I wrote, or feel that prayer is not so important after all. Far from it. But what may be *related* to revival, and what is strictly *relevant* to revival are not one and the same, and there was much in the earlier book that was related rather than relevant. This has been cut in order to keep the book within the compass of a normal paperback, particularly as three new chapters were being added.

People have sometimes asked me, 'Have you changed your convictions about revival since you wrote your first book?' The answer is 'No'. Reading it through after a number of years was a salutary exercise. There were things that I had let slip, and that I needed to hear God speak again to my own heart, but nothing that I wished I had not written. However, *Rain from Heaven* is a *new* book; it is different. This is because I have come to see the importance of revival, not so much in its short-term results for the church, but against the grand back-drop of God's age-long purpose for the church and the world. This has brought a significant change of emphasis.

Thankfully I had never embraced that school of prophetic teaching that sees nothing ahead but things waxing worse and worse, so that the return of Christ becomes an act of intervention to save Christ's 'little flock' from total eclipse. I could never reconcile the promises of the Bible and what I knew of the character of God with such an 'eschatology of disaster'. As a schoolboy I had visited the little Welsh mining village of Loughor, Glamorganshire (with my family), and listened to the stirring tales of what God did in the Revival of 1904. There God lit a flame in my young heart. Whatever anybody said about decline and apostasy in the professing church, the simple and sufficient answer to me was that what God had done before He could do again, and do in our own situation.

In the Day of Thy Power was written over a period of three years. It came out of my experience of the enduement of the Holy Spirit, and out of the ministry I was giving over those years, in churches and conferences, and in the prayer groups that sprang up in the wake of the Lewis Revival of 1950. My mind was full of the need of the church to be revived and renewed, equipped with the power and gifts of the Spirit, and to see the end-time harvest gathered in. All of this I still firmly hold. But the idea of the church's need of reformation and recovery was only then beginning to form in my thinking, and therefore was not strongly emphasised in the first book.

In looking back to those earlier years when much fervent prayer went up for revival, it is the way God answered – the things that He has since done, and, significantly, the things He has *not* done that we expected He would – that have influenced my thinking on the subject of revival. Jesus only did what He saw the Father doing. We too must see where Father is working and what He is doing in our situations, and then work with Him. It is foolish to try to light the flame where the wind of the Spirit is not blowing.

Taking the twenty or more years since my first book was published, I believe the most significant event that has taken place in the church at large has been 'the charismatic movement'. Many within it take it for granted that the movement is in fact the revival of our day. Others, mostly those not identified with it, are equally emphatic that it is not. Though I was involved in the movement from its earliest beginnings, and have never doubted that it was born of God, I do not believe that it was or is revival. The following chapters will explain more fully the reason why. Suffice it to say that while the charismatic movement has certain features that are characteristic of revival, and has accomplished in the church some of the things that are generally attributable to revival, there are nevertheless some indispensable marks of a true outpouring that have been missing, at least as we have experienced it in this country.

'History teaches us,' declared Hegel, 'that history teaches us nothing!' If we do not learn from history, if we do not profit from the mistakes of the past, then we shall be condemned to repeat them. I believe that the charismatic movement is a piece

of contemporary history which has something important to say
to us as we continue to look to God for an outpouring in our
day. In the early years one of the questions that leaders were
asking was, 'How are we to integrate this new life in the Spirit
with our traditional forms of service?' In other words, how can
our historic churches, with their staid and traditional forms of
worship, cope with speaking in tongues and other spiritual
gifts, with the exuberance of charismatic worship, con-
gregational participation, etc?

The simple answer is that they cannot, without radical
change. Apart from a few rare cases, the integration has therefore never been realised. Leaders have not been prepared for
radical change – it is certainly costly – and so the old traditions
and the old structures have proved an insuperable barrier to the
Holy Spirit fully renewing the local church. We find therefore
that many churches who testify to renewal have their 'charismatic thing' on Wednesday night in the Manse, while the rest
of the church, who attend Sunday services and profess to
belong, are left untouched. The new thing that God is doing
was never designed to patch the worn and torn garment of
denominational Christianity. Wine must have a container, but
the old container can never cope with the new wine – unless it is
willing for radical change.

Closely associated with this is a disturbing trend in certain
quarters towards denominational insularity. In the beginning,
as I remember, there was greater openness, greater togetherness
and greater willingness to let denominational loyalty be swal-
lowed up in the greater loyalty to Christ and His one church.
Perhaps at that stage not all had 'thought through' what this
might involve. Now there seems to have come a reaction, at
least on the part of some leaders. Whether we are in old
churches or new churches we must face this fact: God will
never own party spirit or sectional interest. It could well in-
sulate us from the revival that is surely coming.

Though this book emphasises the spiritual rather than the social effects of revival, it is not out of place here to mention that its effect on social reform has been profound. Lecky, the historian, stated that it was the Methodist Revival which saved England from the bloody revolution that overtook France. Writing of the period prior to the American Civil War, Timothy L. Smith, in his *Revivalism and Social Reform*, shows how the curbing of drunkenness, vice and other social ills, as well as the abolition of slavery, were direct results of the revivals that came from the frontier to dominate the urban religious scene.

The message of *Rain from Heaven* is intended to challenge us all for the greater thing that God is waiting to do, and especially those whose personal experience of the Holy Spirit and His gifts tempted them to feel, 'This is it! We are in revival.' I would say again, 'God has something bigger on His heart.' He is ready to give us both the vision of it and the hunger for it. But let us remember that praying for it pre-supposes a willingness for all that it entails. We must be ready for change, for moving on with God, to abandon everything that God shows us is a hindrance, and to embrace whatever new light He causes to break forth from His holy word.

CONTENTS

1. WHAT IS REVIVAL?

Because God is both clothed in majesty and shrouded in mystery, there is something both majestic and mysterious about revival. It is a manifestation of God that bears His own hallmark. This book does not profess to supply all the answers. Could it succeed in doing so, it would probably leave the reader disappointed and disillusioned. The mystery is part of the wonder, and when we lose the sense of wonder we lose the sense of worship. We are not permitted to probe into the secret things that belong to God, but we are to acquaint ourselves with the things that are revealed, for they belong to us and to our children.

What is revival? When used in relation to spiritual things the term conveys widely differing ideas. To the sceptic it conjures up thoughts of excessive emotionalism and mass hysteria. Others use it to describe evangelism. They speak of 'planning a revival' in their church, meaning that they are preparing for an evangelistic drive. Then there are those who believe that it is concerned with the reviving of the people of God rather than reaching the outsider, and who therefore use the term to describe the quickening of believers, or their being filled with the Spirit.

It is true that a powerful revival is inevitably a time of spiritual excitement, but it has nothing to do with hysteria. The lasting results clearly prove that. We need not fear even deep emotion when it is produced by the One who created this capacity within us. It is true that such times involve the salvation of men and women. No revival is complete without this. It is also true that at the heart of such a movement is the quickening of God's people and their being filled with the Holy Spirit. But none of these is, of itself, an adequate definition of what has come to be called down the centuries, 'religious revival'.

It is important that we distinguish revival from evangelism. In evangelism man takes the initiative, though it be with the prompting of the Holy Spirit. In revival the initiative is solely God's. In the one the organisation is human. With the other it is divine. A deep work in the hearts of the Christians is implicit in revival but not necessarily in evangelism. Evangelism there must be – it is part of the continuous programme of the church – but revival is a thing of special times and seasons. Revival may of course break out in the midst of evangelism. In that case certain features will appear that are peculiar to revival, and certain features will disappear that are characteristic of evangelism. While revival tarries evangelism must go on, but let us keep the distinction clear.

Revival then is more than big meetings and great excitement. It is more than a great harvest of converts. It is more than numbers of Christians being revived and filled with the Spirit. One may have any one of these without revival, and yet revival includes them all. Though the Bible does not contain the word revival,[1] it is rich in examples of this phenomenon. We cannot do better than draw our definition from there.

The prophet Habakkuk is praying for a renewing or reviving of God's work.[2] He then proceeds to describe what he sees in vision as the answer to his prayer:

God came . . . His glory covered the heavens, and the earth was full of His praise. His brightness was like the light, rays flashed from His hand; and there He veiled His power.

Only two words, but they touch the heart of the matter – '*God came*'. Taking the inspired prophet as our guide, we may say that revival is a visitation of God and the characteristic features are 'His glory', 'His praise', 'His hand' (symbolic of the Holy Spirit),[3] 'His power'.

What do we mean by 'a visitation of God'? And how is this idea to be reconciled with the omnipresence of God? Certainly God is everywhere,[4] but it is still true that He is in some places in a way that He is not everywhere. He is in the hearts of those who love Him in a way that He is not in the hearts of those who hate Him. In His heavenly habitation He 'dwells in unapproachable light'[5] in a way that He could not dwell among even His greatest saints on earth. So when we speak of God visiting His people, we mean that He comes to them in a manifestation of His power and glory that is far beyond anything they normally experience.

Revival then is such a display of God's holiness and power that often human personalities are overshadowed and human programmes abandoned. It is God breaking into the consciousness of men in majesty and glory. Isaiah, faced with a people who had rebelled and grieved God's Holy Spirit, pleads for such a manifestation:

O that Thou wouldst rend the heavens and come down, that the mountains might quake at Thy presence . . . to make Thy name known to Thy adversaries, and that the nations might tremble at Thy presence![6]

Many another Old Testament prophet living in dark days found a ray of hope in the expectation of such a visitation.

When we turn to the New Testament such times are seen to be directly related to the pouring out of the Holy Spirit. As the birthday of the church Pentecost was unique, but as a specimen outpouring of the Spirit it was only unique in being the first.

Peter recognised in that dramatic event the fulfilment of Joel's prophecy spoken centuries before. Now what Joel had actually said was, 'It shall come to pass *afterward*, that I will pour out My Spirit.'[7] But Peter, in quoting him, is inspired to change this to, '*In the last days* it shall be ... that I will pour out My Spirit.'[8]

Joel's promise of the outpouring of the Spirit refers therefore *to a period of time*, 'the last days', and is not to be confined to *a point of time* such as the day of Pentecost. This is further confirmed by the fact that Joel's prophecy quoted by Peter was only partially fulfilled on the day of Pentecost. There was evidently more to come. In fact, the prophecy seems to stretch right on to the period immediately prior to 'the day of the Lord'.[9] From God's standpoint the whole age of the church constitutes 'the last days', so we should not be surprised to find subsequent examples of this kind of visitation in the Acts record, notably that which took place in Caesarea, which Luke describes as a pouring out of the gift of the Holy Spirit.[10] Similarly, Paul, who did not experience the outpouring at Pentecost or at Caesarea, uses the same expression when he reminds Titus of their own experience: 'The Holy Spirit, which He poured out upon *us* richly.'[11]

Since New Testament days every true revival that has blessed the church has been marked by powerful and often widespread outpourings of the Spirit. Jonathan Edwards, whom God used powerfully in New England in the early eighteenth century, put it clearly if somewhat quaintly when he said,

God hath it much on His heart from all eternity to glorify His dear and only begotten Son; and there are some special seasons that He appoints to that end, wherein He comes forth with omnipotent power to fulfil His promise and oath to Him. And these times are times of remarkable pouring out of

His Spirit to advance His kingdom. Such a day is a day of
His power.

David Brainerd recorded the beginning of the wonderful
movement among the American Indians in 1745 in these
words,

> The power of God seemed to descend upon the assembly like
> a mighty rushing wind and with an astonishing energy bore
> down all before it. I stood amazed at the influence that
> seized the audience almost universally, and could compare it
> to nothing more aptly than the irresistible force of a mighty
> torrent.

Who would deny that this was an outpouring of the Holy
Spirit? Who could find words more appropriate to describe it
than those of Luke, 'The Holy Spirit fell on all who heard the
word'?[12]

Revival can never be explained in terms of activity or organisation, personality or preaching. Whether or not they are involved, they cannot account for the effects produced. It is
essentially a manifestation of God. It has the stamp of deity
upon it, and this even the spiritually uninitiated are quick to
recognise. We cannot explain revival because we cannot explain God. 'The wind blows where it wills.' Though we do not
understand its vagaries we may still 'trim the sail' and work
with it. To move with God in the day of His power means
understanding and conforming to those principles by which He
has chosen to work.

NOTES

1. Only 'revive' and 'reviving' are found in our common versions
2. Hab. 3:2–4
3. Cf. Ezek. 8:1 with 11:5
4. Ps. 139:7–10
5. 1 Tim:6.16
6. Isa. 64:1–2
7. Joel 2:28 both Hebrew and Greek LXX text
8. Acts 2:17
9. Acts 2:20
10. Acts 10:45
11. Titus 3:5–6
12. Acts 10:44

2. A SIGN SPOKEN AGAINST

Speak about revival, and if people know what you are talking about, you will have a variety of reactions. Some respond with enthusiasm, for they have the hope burning within them. Some are stolidly indifferent; they don't wish to be disturbed. While others again are opposed to the whole concept.

> Behold, this child is set for the fall and rising of many in Israel, and for a sign that is spoken against . . . that thoughts out of many hearts may be revealed.[1]

So spoke the aged Simeon as he held baby Jesus in his arms. The prophecy began to be fulfilled thirty years later as Christ stood in his own synagogue of Nazareth and began to read from the roll of the book. When He applied the message in power to the hearts of His hearers their initial wonder gave place to anger, and soon they were trying to do away with Him over the city cliff. As soon as He began to move in the power of the Spirit He became a stone of stumbling that would cause 'the fall and rising of many in Israel'; He became 'a sign that is spoken against', revealing the true condition of many hearts.

It has been so with every servant of God whose ministry was endued with power. It has been so with every movement of the Spirit which has blessed the church. It has been so with every true revival – 'a sign that is spoken against', that uncovers the hidden thoughts of the heart. The powerful operation of the Spirit will always draw forth the antagonism of the carnal mind which is 'hostile to God'. Those whom God singles out to be His instruments may expect to be the targets. Satan never seems to lack willing hands and lips to do His work, in the professing church as well as out of it.

Many know of the way God used Jonathan Edwards in the New England Awakening, but few that he was compelled to resign from the church so signally blessed under his ministry. Many have heard of William Burns, under whose ministry God came to Murray McCheyne's church in Dundee, but few know of the gruelling he received in defending that work before a panel of his fellow-ministers. So it was with Finney and many others. Find a revival that is not spoken against and you need to look again to be sure that it is a revival.

Some speak against it out of ignorance. They have never themselves experienced it, and what they have heard or read has been strongly biased. Just a taste of the real thing, or an openness to receive the testimony of those who have themselves tasted it, would go a long way towards relieving them of their fears and prejudices.

Many are afraid of excesses, divisions, or other undesirable features. It is true that these do occur. No one would pretend that every revival burns with a smokeless flame. But let us test the argument. Was the first church at Jerusalem wrong to have sold their possessions and given to those in need because of the sordid case of Ananias and Sapphira? Should not the young churches have celebrated the Communion because this was abused at Corinth? Ought there to have been no Reformation because sometimes excesses and wrongs were perpetrated?

After drought, the copious rains often deluge the land, and sweep away bridges, and otherwise do very much harm. But no one is so alarmed by the evils of rain, as to desire a continuation of the drought.[2]

The picture must be seen in perspective, and any evils must be weighed against the overall good.

Some are deeply desirous of such a visitation until it comes, and then they bitterly oppose it because it did not come as they had anticipated. Either the instrument God used or the channel through which the blessing flowed was contrary to their expectations. They looked for an Eliab or an Abinadab, and God, who looks on the heart, chose a David. They thought that *their* church, which was so scriptural and spiritual, would be the scene of the visitation, but God chose to work elsewhere. What a need there is to guard against pride, prejudice, and jealousy!

Often people are stumbled by the manner of the Spirit's working. God exhibited His power in a manner that was contrary to their expectation or new to their experience, and this became a stumbling-block. Just as the Jews rejected their Messiah because He did not conform to their preconceived ideas, so these people reject the manifestation of God. Jonathan Edwards witnessed this mistake being made two hundred years ago, and wrote:

Persons are very ready to be suspicious of what they have not felt themselves. It is to be feared many good men have been guilty of this error ... These persons that thus make their own experience their rule of judgment, instead of bowing to the wisdom of God, and yielding to to His word as an infallible rule, are guilty of casting a great reflection upon the understanding of the Most High.

Thus a movement of the Spirit becomes a sign spoken against, and those who thus speak inevitably reveal the thoughts of their hearts.

There are many earnest people who do not speak against revival – they believe if it came it would do much good – but against the *expectation* of it. We are at the end of the age, they remind us, and Scripture has predicted that perilous times shall come, and that things in the world are to get worse and worse. How, then, can we look for such blessing? But it was in grievous and perilous times that the church was born. God evidently found it necessary then to pour out His Spirit. And if the age is to be consummated in an even greater time of world turmoil, how much *more* needful that God should again intervene in power to complete His church and vindicate His name. Is there widespread rejection of God's law? Then, according to the Psalmist, 'It is time for the Lord to act.'[3]

History shows that man's desperate plight has again and again called forth all the mightier working of God. Revival demonstrates God's readiness to retrieve what was humanly hopeless. In addition to this, we have been warned that the end of the age is to be marked by deception through Satanic signs and wonders.[4] Do we expect God to withhold His hand and give the devil the monopoly in the realm of the supernatural? Are 'the magicians of Egypt' to turn their rods into serpents while Moses and Aaron stand helplessly by? Should we not expect God's servants to do as much, and more, that their rods should swallow up those of the magicians, according to the promise, 'He who is in you is greater than he who is in the world'?[5]

There are others that argue that revival must begin *in the church*, but that the Scriptures predict that *in the church* prior to Christ's return there is to be a falling away, that the love of the many will wax cold, and the Laodicean spirit will prevail. These things are already happening, they tell us; how then can we expect such a movement of the Spirit? What a remarkable memory some believers have for all the gloomy predictions of Scripture! As soon as there is a mention of revival they clutch after them in a desperate bid to preserve the status quo, forgetting that such warnings must be balanced by the many promises of hope. I feel that I want to quote Paul to such people, 'May *the God of hope* fill you with all joy and peace in believing, so that by the power of the Holy Spirit *you may abound in hope*.'[6]

The answer to this quite common view is to be found in the understanding of the purpose of prophecy. Whether the church of Laodicea represents the last epoch of church history is a matter of prophetic interpretation, and we need not concern ourselves with it here. We only need to ask, Has Christ presented us with the picture of Laodicea as an example to follow or a state to condone? Did He intend that we should resign ourselves fatalistically to the spirit of Laodicea because we believe that we are in the end times? The Lord warned this church that its lukewarmness would result in judgment unless there was repentance.[7] Surely His purpose in this whole message was that the church might be moved to repent, and so be delivered from its lukewarmness and the judgment He had pronounced upon it.

When Jonah predicted the overthrow of Nineveh, the nation repented. We then read, 'God repented of the evil which He had said He would do to them; and He did not do it'.[8] When Daniel brought to Nebuchadnezzar a warning of impending judgment, he did not advise him meekly to await his punishment, but counselled him to break off his sins, to show mercy to the poor, that perhaps God might lengthen his days of peace.[9] Israel's history of decline, though foreseen by God and predicted by the prophets, was not an unalterable decree. In the midst of the decline there were a number of remarkable movements of the Spirit, when godly kings and fearless prophets turned the people back to God.

If lukewarmness and apostasy are predicted for the endtime, it is surely not that we might apathetically await the fulfilment, but that we may be forewarned and strive to avert it. This would inevitably create in our hearts a desire for God to come in power. There is nothing more calculated to arrest the downward trend, and set a lukewarm church on fire, than a true awakening of the Holy Spirit. So these very prophecies that objectors use should produce in the heart of every believer, not a dumb resignation to fate, but a fervent desire for a movement of God. 'Many are saying, "Who will show us any good?" Lift up the light of Thy countenance upon us, O Lord!'[10]

But some will still object, believing that the church should not be looking for revival, but for the return of Christ. Of course Christians should be looking for Christ's return, but are they? Hardly, when carnality, apathy, and worldliness are so rife. But such a state is incompatible with a people preparing and praying for God to come in power. A church ready for revival is a church ready for His coming. They have purified themselves, and John tells us that it is this purifying that is the indispensable preparation for Christ's return, and the final proof that we really have the hope within us.[11]

When we consider the effect of revival on the church, there is no better preparation for Christ's return than a true visitation of the Holy Spirit. In *Rent Heavens* R. B. Jones records that, prior to the 1904 Awakening in Wales, there was hardly a pulpit in the principality where the truth of Christ's personal advent was preached. Then the revival came, and with it a great light. He records how the truth one day flashed into his own heart without having heard or read anything on the subject, 'that the Lord was coming; that He was coming quickly; that indeed He *must* come; and that apart from His coming there seemed no hope for the world'.

If we admit that the church is in a sleepy state the argument in favour of 'an awakening', as a revival is often called, grows stronger as the end of the age approaches. At least Paul seemed to think so, when he said,

It is full time now for you to wake from sleep. For salvation is nearer to us now than when we first believed; the night is far gone, the day is at hand. Let us then cast off the works of darkness and put on the armour of light.[12]

The hope of spiritual awakening is not a substitute but a supplement to the hope of His coming. Indeed the promise that He is to appear for 'those who are eagerly waiting for Him'[13] must surely make revival imperative.

Of course the final answer to these objections is the answer of facts. If it is true that God is not willing to pour out His Spirit because He has predicted something different for these end-times, and we need rather to be watching for Christ's return, then the argument must be true universally and continuously and without exception. We cannot apply it to Britain, but not to Indonesia; to North America but not to South America. Anyone who has studied the subject will know that the out-pouring of the Spirit is, and always has been, a constantly re-curring phenomenon in different parts of the world. God has given us abundant evidence of this, right up to the present time. There have been wonderful outpourings in many parts of South America, in Korea, in Indonesia, and in many other lands. These give the lie to the suggestion that God is not willing because we are nearing the end of the day of grace.

The simple fact that God is still doing it today is the strongest argument against every objection. When God poured out His spirit in the house of Cornelius, some narrow-minded people in Jerusalem thought it was all wrong: it ought never to have been. But when Peter told his story every objector was silenced, and instead of carping they glorified God. Let us spread abroad the news of what God is doing. Nothing fans the flame of faith for such a divine visitation as up-to-date news that God is still in the business.

Men shall proclaim the might of Thy terrible acts,
  And I will declare Thy greatness.
They shall pour forth the fame of Thy abundant goodness,
  And shall sing aloud of Thy righteousness.[14]

NOTES

1. Luke 2:34–35
2. Wm. Patton, DD
3. Ps. 119:126
4. Matt. 24:24; 2 Thess. 2:9–11
5. 1 John 4:4
6. Rom. 15:13
7. Rev. 3:16, 19
8. Jonah 3:10
9. Dan. 4:27
10. Ps. 4:6 NASB
11 1 John 3:3
12. Rom. 13:11–12
13. Heb. 9:28
14. Ps. 145:6–7

3. THE PROMISED RAIN

'What are the prospects of revival?' I asked. 'They are as bright as the promises of God,' was the swift reply. Twenty years have passed, but my friend's reply is as relevant as ever. We know there are to be those who will question the hope of Christ's return, and ask, 'Where is the promise of His Coming?'[1] Even so there are those who ask, 'Where is the promise of revival?' Does the Scripture hold out solid ground for such a great expectation?

The awakenings that have blessed the church in days gone by have usually come in response to the cries of a praying remnant. Were their prayers based on optimism or wishful thinking? We have only to consider the way God responded to find our answer. Since we have no right to expect God to do what He has not promised to do, their prayers must surely have been based on the promises of God's word. Prior to the Lewis Awakening of 1949 in the Outer Hebrides, there was a small band of determined intercessors who were led to plead that promise, 'I will pour water upon him that is thirsty, and floods upon the dry ground.'[2]

Perhaps these simple Hebridean crofters had not been told that it was quite inappropriate to apply Israel promises to the church! I don't suppose they had ever heard of modern dispensational teaching. Of one thing they were sure, God had quickened this scripture to their hearts. It seemed to them heaven's answer to the desperate spiritual need they saw on every hand. Consequently they pleaded that promise until the Holy Spirit came. Such promises of a visitation in power – and there are many of them in the Old Testament prophets – have so often provided the biblical basis of such praying. Judging by the way God has answered, He never intended these Old Testament promises to be confined to dispensational pigeon-holes.

Revival praying, as we have already seen, is closely linked with the New Testament promise of the Holy Spirit. There have always been those who have argued that praying for the Holy Spirit was unscriptural. Jeremiah Meneely was one of the four young men of that famous Kells prayer meeting in Northern Ireland out of which sprang the Ulster 1859 Awakening. Towards the end of his life he recalled how some had in those early days discouraged them in their praying for the pouring out of the Holy Spirit, arguing that they already had the Holy Spirit. They were not to be put off but, as Meneely put it, 'We just kept on praying until the power came.'

In the midst of his second great sermon, following the healing of the lame man at the gate of the Temple, Peter declares:

> Repent therefore, and turn again, that your sins may be blotted out, that times of refreshing may come from the presence of the Lord, and that He may send the Christ appointed for you, Jesus.[3]

Here revivals are well described as 'times of refreshing . . . from the presence of the Lord'. Here in brief is the three-fold purpose of God for His people. It begins with repentance and a turning to God; then, times of refreshing; and finally, the return of Christ. Here then, is solid New Testament ground for seasons of blessing before Christ comes back. Peter had just witnessed the age of the Spirit being ushered in with Pentecostal showers. He now tells us that this age is to be marked, right up to the promised return of Christ, with such 'times of refreshing'.

To the oriental mind, time of refreshing would suggest the coming of the rain after the long dry season. Rain is a continual picture throughout Scripture of the outpouring of the Holy Spirit. Before the Israelites had entered their inheritance, Moses described to them the land of Canaan,

> The land which you are going over to possess is a land of hills and valleys, which drinks water by the rain from heaven ... And if you will obey My commandments ... to love the Lord your God, and to serve Him with all your heart and with all your soul, He will give the rain for your land in its season, the early rain and the later rain, that you may gather in your grain and your wine and your oil.[4]

This reminds us that Israel's harvest was dependent on the rain, and the rain in turn was dependent on Israel loving and obeying God.

The rainy season usually commences in the land of Israel about the end of October with light showers that soften the ground. It continues with heavy intermittent falls often lasting two or three days throughout November and December. These heavier falls, called the former or early rain, soften the soil for ploughing and sowing. Lesser showers then continue intermittently, for at no point during the winter do they completely cease. Then throughout April and early May the heavy showers return. This was known as the latter or later rain, meaning the rain of ingathering, for it served to swell the grain for the harvest.

The similarity between this rainy season and the age of the Spirit is striking. We see in the ministries of John the Baptist and Jesus, when multitudes heard the message of the kingdom,[5] the first soft showers that heralded the time of rain.

These told all those 'looking for the consolation of Israel' that the long season of drought was over, and that the time of rain had come. At the outset of His ministry Jesus said, 'You shall see greater things than these,'[6] and at its conclusion, 'Greater works than these will (you) do.'[7] Those heavy showers of the former rain commenced to fall at Pentecost, when God poured out His Spirit in fulfilment of Joel's prophecy. Outpourings continued throughout that first century, gradually diminishing in power and frequency as faith and spirituality declined.

Through the ensuing centuries the showers continued here and there, now and again, though the heavier downpourings of revival were few and far between. Since the Reformation these have been more distinct and frequent. Jesus Himself told us, 'The harvest is the close of the age,'[8] that is, the time of His return. Surely then we are in the time of the latter rain, when the fruit of the earth is being prepared for the final harvest.

In striking confirmation of this is the exhortation of James:

> Be patient, therefore, brethren, until the coming of the Lord. Behold, the farmer waits for the precious fruit of the earth, being patient over it until it receives the early and the late rain. You also be patient. Establish your hearts, for the coming of the Lord is at hand.[9]

In using the illustration of the farmer, he, too, likens the coming of the Lord to harvest time. But waiting for the harvest involves waiting for the early and late rain that precedes it, and helps produce it. Interpreting the analogy, waiting in expectation for the coming of the Lord means waiting in expectation for the promised outpouring that will surely usher it in.

All this lends great weight to that word of one of the last Old Testament prophets Zechariah, 'Ask rain from the Lord in the season of the spring (or latter) rain, from the Lord ... who gives them showers of rain'.[10] Just as there is a season for the latter rain, so there is a time for the latter day outpouring of the Spirit. I believe that God is showing an increasing number of His children that that time is *now*. If we are not sure, let us seek Him for revelation; if we are, then let us heed this word of counsel. Though it is the season for the promised rain, we are not to fold our arms and wait passively for it to come; we are to call on the Lord to send it. It could well be that this latter rain, when it is manifested in its fullness, will prove to be a world-wide outpouring, exceeding anything that the church in its long history has ever seen.

NOTES

1. 2 Pet. 3:4
2. Isa. 44:3 AV
3. Acts 3:19–20
4. Deut. 11:11, 13–14
5. Matt. 3:5; 4:25
6. John 1:50
7. John 14:12
8. Matt. 13:39
9. Jas. 5:7–8
10. Zech. 10:1RV

4. THIS IS THE PURPOSE

Since the dawn of human history God has caused His purposes to progress by sudden and powerful movements of His Spirit. Take the Flood, the Exodus and the entry of Canaan in the Old Testament; or the Day of Pentecost in the New. While acknowledging this to be so, we may well ask why God has chosen to work in this way. Would it not have been more satisfactory had His work progressed quietly and steadily, without these times of spiritual upheaval? The title 'Lord of Hosts (Armies)' reminds us that God is a military commander, and His ways in revival disclose something of His heavenly strategy. He uses these times to *counteract spiritual decline*, and then to *create spiritual momentum*.

Had the work of God's kingdom advanced steadily and consistently down the centuries, presumably visitations of the Spirit would not have been necessary. But this has never been the case. Decline and decay, inherent in human nature, are not confined to the physical and moral realm, but appear in the spiritual also. We see it in the history of Israel. We see it in New Testament times. We see it in the subsequent history of the church. God has seen fit to counteract this ever-present tendency by seizing the initiative, and working at times in unusual power. In this way ground has been recovered from the enemy, and the spiritual equilibrium restored.

History shows that when the Spirit of God is working in this way, the results are usually deep and abiding. Those thus converted or revived are, on the whole, more likely to go on with God than is the case at other times. The generation that has never seen a display of God's power is more likely to go the way of the world than the generation that has witnessed such a mighty work of God. Witness the history of Israel in the time of the Judges:

> And the people served the Lord all the days of Joshua, and all the days of the elders who outlived Joshua, *who had seen all the great work which the Lord had done* for Israel . . . and there arose another generation after them, *who did not know the Lord or the work which He had done* for Israel. And the people of Israel did what was evil in the sight of the Lord and served the Baals.[1]

It would not make for the spiritual health of God's people if these displays of God's power were other than occasional, just as it would not make for a healthy crop if it was subjected to a continuous deluge for the whole of its growing life. Nevertheless, when the work of God is in decline there is nothing calculated to recover the situation so speedily and effectively as such a visitation of the Holy Spirit. In the very nature of things revival presupposes declension.

Time and again spiritual situations that seemed beyond recovery have been transformed when God has intervened in this way. One recalls D. M. Panton's pithy definition of revival as 'the inrush of the Spirit into a body that threatens to become a corpse'.

God also uses an outpouring to create spiritual momentum. When the people of God are 'in the doldrums' and when the still air of lethargy and inertia hangs over the work of the king-

dom, there is a need for God to blow with His wind. Then what
is static suddenly bursts into spiritual life and motion, and the
work of God moves forward with power.

There is a military principle known as *concentration of force*
by which a commander will husband his reserves and con-
centrate them at a strategic point for the sudden strike. He will
hope to break through the enemy defences and so pave the way
for a general advance. A powerful thrust of this sort may well
achieve what harassing the enemy or even attacking him on a
broad front fails to accomplish. In the same way revival will
effect what the quieter workings of the Spirit do not.

A reservoir in the hills supplied a village community with
water. It was fed by a mountain stream, and the overflow from
the reservoir continued down the stream-bed to the valley
below. This stream never attracted any attention or gave the
villagers any trouble. One day, however, some large cracks appeared in one of the walls of the old reservoir. Soon afterwards
the wall collapsed, and the water came cascading down the
hillside. Great trees were rooted up, boulders tossed about like
playthings, houses and bridges destroyed. What had before
been taken for granted now became an object of awe and
wonder and fear. From far and near people came to see what
had happened.

This is the kind of picture language that Scripture uses to
describe the strategic move of God we call revival:

So they shall fear the name of the Lord from the west, and
His glory from the rising of the sun; for He will come like a
rushing stream, which the wind of the Lord drives.[2]

Often preceding such times the stream of blessing has been
unusually low. But in response to the prayers of a faithful remnant God has been heaping the flood. Then when few have any
expectation of it, God releases the flood of blessing. Or some-

times it comes like the river of the sanctuary seen in Ezekiel's vision, commencing insignificantly, only ankle-deep, but soon becoming, in the full tide of blessing, deep enough to swim in.

In this way the work of God becomes an object of awe and wonder. Strongholds of Satan which have long resisted the normal influences of the Spirit are swept away. Stubborn wills that have long withstood the pressure of the gospel bend and break before the irresistible flow of the Spirit, to be themselves engulfed and carried along in the stream of blessing. In this way God uses revival to accomplish, sometimes in a few days, what could never have been achieved even in years of normal Christian activity.

A word of warning is necessary here. We must be careful not to disparage the quieter seasons, for God has His purpose in these times also. The reconnoitring and patrolling, the harassing and skirmishing are all essential to the big offensive. The day of small things is preparatory and supplementary to the day of God's power, and we must not despise it.

However, history teaches us that most of the great forward movements of the church have been born in seasons of spiritual awakening. For example, the great missionary advance of the last century derived its momentum from the widespread revivals that blessed America and Britain during those years. In fact, ever since the light was almost eclipsed in medieval times, God has been working to restore to the church the purity, the power and the knowledge of His ways that are its birthright. God is after the recovery of a full-orbed New Testament Christianity, and as we shall see in a later chapter, He has invariably used revivals to this end.

Notes

1. Judges 2:7–11
2. Isa. 59:19

5. HOW SET IN MOTION

Pentecost, as the first distinctive outpouring of the Spirit, reveals the characteristics of every subsequent outpouring. In the next few chapters we shall be looking at these, using Acts 2 as our text book. But first let us consult this great chapter on the controversial question of how revival is set in motion. Is it simply a sovereign act of God without regard to human factors, such as the spiritual state of those who experience it? Or does it come inevitably when God finds some people who will obey certain laws or fulfil certain conditions? These two questions suggest opposite and seemingly irreconcilable views that Christians have held over the years.

Every revival *is* certainly a sovereign act of God, but this is not to say that it is exercised without regard to the spiritual response of His people. It is a mistake to view the sovereignty of God, as some Calvinists seem to do, as the hub of the Deity, with all God's other attributes radiating like spokes from the hub. God's sovereignty (or ability to do what He wills) is clearly subordinate to His character of holiness and love. Because He is a moral being and has constituted man a moral being, He cannot act without reference to His moral principles. Even a sovereign God cannot forgive the unrepentant or bless the disobedient.

Though man may be influenced from within and from without, God still holds him responsible for his moral choices. This is the consistent teaching of Scripture, and we must not weaken the grasp on conscience that this provides by suggesting that since the Fall man is no longer a free agent, no longer with a will of his own. This view, carried to its logical conclusion, not only has a tendency to absolve the unconverted person from his moral responsibility towards God, but by the same token to relieve the believer of his responsibility in terms of obedience and submission. Both could be tempted to take up a passive attitude and leave it to the God who 'works all things according to the purpose of His will'.

While acknowledging that Scripture gives some place to man's responsibility in the matter of a spiritual outpouring, it would surely be erroneous to suggest that the blessing inevitably follows when God's people fulfil certain conditions. That would be taking the initiative out of God's hands and placing it in the hands of men. It would mean that man could release the power of revival as and when he chose, just as one of the great powers could release on the world a holocaust of nuclear power at the touch of a button. History shows that revival does not come in such a mechanical way. When, in trying to explain it, we have taken all the known factors into account we are still left with the element of mystery. We can only exclaim with Paul, 'How unsearchable are His judgments and how inscrutable His ways!'[1]

In the case of the Pentecost outpouring, we have an allusion to the sovereign will and timing of God, 'When the day of Pentecost had come'; then, in the same breath, a clear reference to a work of spiritual preparation in the hearts of the waiting band, 'They were all together in one place.'[2] The two factors, God's sovereignty and man's responsibility, are presented side by side. We are not required to try to reconcile them, any more than the Bible does. The truth is not to be found in one or the other but in both. When we hold them in tension, as Scripture

does, we shall hold the truth in balance. Otherwise we shall
omit something important of the counsel of God.

Notice how this hallmark of divine sovereignty is seen in the
time factor, 'When the day of Pentecost had come.' There was a
moment for that first outpouring determined, not by the believers in the upper room, but by the Lord in heaven. The feast of
Pentecost[3] was an annual event held fifty days (hence the name
Pentecost, meaning fifty) after the offering of the barley sheaf
at the time of the Passover.

These Old Testament feasts had a prophetic significance,
and prophecy must have its fulfilment. The God who had
arranged that His Son should be offered up as the sacrificial
lamb at the Passover season, also saw to it that the Spirit should
be poured out fifty days after He rose from the dead, to fulfil
the Feast of Pentecost. This is why that great day could never
have come sooner than it did, no matter how earnestly the disciples had prayed or prepared their hearts.

God had also foreseen that the day of Pentecost would be a
strategic moment to give to the event of that day the maximum
possible effect. The assembling in Jerusalem of 'Jews, devout
men from every nation under heaven'[4] for the annual feast
ensured that the repercussions would be felt throughout the
world of that day. Even the hour was appointed by God so that
the mocking charge that these people were drunk might easily
be refuted, since it was only nine o'clock in the morning.[5]

Similarly, God has His time for every subsequent outpouring of His Spirit, and in the very nature of things this must
be related to a thousand other plans He has in hand. We have
already noticed that God promised Israel rain in the land of
Canaan, but only 'in its season'.[6] God alone determines when it
is time for rain. It has been said of the Welsh Revival at the
beginning of the century, 'The outpouring of the Spirit came
dramatically with precision, in the second week in November

1904, on the same day – both in the north and in the south.'
There is no accounting for this remarkable co-ordination apart
from the divine strategy that lies behind the sovereign ways of
God.

A sober view of God's sovereignty will never discourage fervent praying in the Spirit, but it may well deliver us from
presumption on the one hand: thinking that God is under command; and from discouragement on the other: when God does
not work as and when we think He should. Revival, as we have
said, is a strategic move by the armies of heaven against the
forces of Satan. The 'when' and 'how' and 'through whom' of
such a move is not determined by the soldier in the field, but by
the commander-in-chief at headquarters. We must bow to the
sovereign will of God not only in the matter of the timing of
every movement, but in the manner and measure of the Spirit's
working.

Then there was the hallmark of spiritual preparation. When
God's hour struck on that memorable day the disciples 'were all
together in one place'. This suggests that they were in a complete state of preparedness. How they had reached this is shown
in the previous chapter where we find that 'all ... with one
accord devoted themselves to prayer'.[7] It may be said that this
was so because God was at work within them. True, but He was
not at work within them without their willing co-operation.
The spiritual history of these disciples had uncovered quite a
good deal of carnality, self-seeking, and petty squabbling. If, as
may well have been the case, they had been exhorting one
another to self-humbling, repentance, and confession in the
light of their Master's promise to send the Holy Spirit, they
were not thereby guilty of taking things out of God's hands, but
were rightly co-operating with Him in the outworking of His
plan.

So Pentecost was marked by the sovereignty of God and by
the preparedness of man. We may not be able to explain how

they harmonise, but because they are both factors in a movement of the Spirit we accept them without question. Some have so exaggerated divine sovereignty as to argue, 'If God wills to send revival it will come. Nothing we do can affect this, so why bother?' Such an attitude is fatalistic and irresponsible, and cannot be supported by the teaching of Scripture. No less harmful is the overemphasis on man's part which I have already mentioned. It ignores the fact of divine sovereignty by implying that God is at our beck and call, and that we can secure an outpouring any day we care to pay the price.

It is true there are spiritual conditions attached to every spiritual blessing. It is right that we should emphasise the importance of repenting, of obeying God, of seeking His face, but we must not consider that we 'buy' revival in this way, or that when we have done all those things that are commanded, God will immediately respond with a powerful outpouring of His Spirit. Charles Finney in his *Lectures On Revival* suggested that we could promote revival just as a farmer promoted a harvest, by ploughing his land and sowing his seed. The analogy is valid if we remember, that despite the most diligent preparation, the crop may fail because of other factors.

History teaches us that though there is always blessing when God's people humble themselves and seek God's face, it does not always or immediately secure that powerful intervention of God we call revival. God has never stated in His word that a certain number of prepared hearts are necessary before the blessing will fall. Sometimes a number have sought God's face with clean hands and pure hearts, but there was only a measure of blessing which did not spread to any great degree. At other times when there was but a handful of prepared and praying people, there was a powerful visitation which spread like a prairie fire. It is impossible to equate the depth and extent of initial preparation with the depth and extent of resultant blessing.

Having said all that, we are still obliged to heed the many exhortations to humble ourselves, clear the ground for God's working, and earnestly seek His powerful intervention. More will be said about this in a subsequent chapter. The fact is that what have been called 'conditions for revival' are basically no different to conditions for any other spiritual blessing. God never puts a premium on carelessness or disobedience by divorcing His promises from human responsibility. Whatever God may be pleased to do in a sovereign way and seemingly without regard to the spiritual state of His people, is His concern. The fact remains, if we are to judge by what He has said in His word, we have no right to expect Him to intervene in the face of our indifference, disobedience and prayerlessness.

NOTES

1. Rom. 11:33
2. Acts 2:1
3. Also known as the Feast of 'Harvest', of 'Firstfruits' or of 'Weeks', because held seven weeks and a day (50 days) after the Passover. Exod. 23:16; 34. 22. Lev. 23:15–16
4. Acts 2:5
5. Acts 2:15
6. Deut. 11:14; cf. Ezek. 34:26
7. Acts 1:14

6. SUDDENLY FROM HEAVEN

Luke describes the Pentecostal outpouring as coming 'suddenly . . . from heaven'.[1] This suggests two important features. There is the mark of *suddenness*. We have already seen that God is a man of war and a superb strategist. He makes use of the surprise element by striking suddenly. Revival overtakes men, comes upon them, catches them unawares. When men fear that God is about to corner them and confront them with His claims, they tend to take avoiding action. But in revival God often moves so swiftly that they are pierced with conviction before they know what has happened.

God will shoot His arrow at them; they will be wounded *suddenly* . . . Then all men will fear; they will tell what God has wrought, and ponder what He has done.[2]

An unusual revival took place in the reign of King Hezekiah. The house of the Lord was cleansed from the gross idolatry that had marked the previous reign. This was followed by a spontaneous move on the part of the people to offer sacrifices and thank-offerings. So abundant was their response that the priests had to call for the help of the Levites to handle all the offerings. The record states: 'Hezekiah and all the people rejoiced because of what God had done for the people; for the thing came about *suddenly*.'[3]

This surprise element in the operation of the Spirit on the day of Pentecost is clear from the reactions of the crowds who were drawn to where God was working. 'They were bewildered ... they were amazed and wondered.'[4] Surprise of this kind invariably brings with it the fear of God, even among the careless and indifferent, and paves the way for a deep work of the Holy Spirit.

But it is not only the outsider that is taken unawares – often a slumbering church is surprised by a sudden awakening of the Spirit. Charles Finney used to describe with a touch of humour how in a time of revival believers 'would wake up all of a sudden, like a man just rubbing his eyes open and running round the room pushing things over, and wondering where all this excitement came from'.

Scripture repeatedly warns us that we are not to be found sleeping when Christ returns, but watching and waiting. If that day overtakes us as a thief in the night we shall suffer serious loss. For the same reason we must not be found unprepared for the Spirit's visitation. God always speaks beforehand to those who have ears to hear and reveals to them what He is about to do. He may have to pull back His servants from the rush and bustle of Christian activity to share with them His secret plan. 'Behold, the former things have come to pass, and new things I now declare; before they spring forth I tell you of them.'[5]

I have already mentioned how revival broke out suddenly in North and South Wales in November 1904. Though it took many by surprise there were those as always in the watchtower of prayer, with whom God had been pleased to share the secret of what He was about to do. They had heard the 'sound of marching'. They had seen the rising of the 'little cloud like a man's hand'. They were praying with expectant faith, fully assured that what God had promised, He was able to perform. When revival came they were ready. This is invariably the case with every movement of the Spirit. Let us ask God to give us the listening ear and the sensitive spirit that the day of visitation may find us ready also.

'Suddenly ... *from heaven.*' There is no feature of revival more important for us to understand than that which is conveyed by the two words, '*from heaven*'. Here is the hallmark of the real thing as distinct from that which men commonly call 'revival', but which may be 'organised', 'promoted', and so presumably controlled. Did anyone organise, promote or control that which came from heaven on the day of Pentecost? Only God. Certainly not the men of 'the upper room prayer meeting'.

Revival is spontaneous in the sense that it is 'not forced or suggested or caused by outside agency' (Oxford Dictionary). It is the result of a divine and not a human impulse. In plainest language, it cannot be 'worked up'. This is not to imply, as I have already said, that revival does not call for spiritual preparation. We have already seen that promises of revival are scattered throughout the Book. And invariably we find that God's promises have God's conditions attached to them. But fulfilled conditions do not provide the motive force of revival. On the day of Pentecost it was 'the windows of heaven' that were opened. The source of blessing was the heart of God rather than the heart of man. 'Times of refreshing' have always come 'from the presence of the Lord'.[6] Trace the river of blessing to its source and you are back, beyond human factors and fulfilled conditions, to God Himself. It is the heart of the Eternal that yearns to bless, and to bless superabundantly.

The rain of Canaan pictures accurately this very feature of revival. Egypt, which stands for the world and its ways, is contrasted with Canaan, which speaks of that which is heavenly:

For the land which you are entering to take possession of it is not like the land of Egypt, from which you have come, where you sowed your seed and watered it with your feet, like a

garden of vegetables; but the land which you are going over
to possess is a land of hills and valleys, which drinks water
by the rain from heaven.[7]

What a contrast Israel was to face when the home they had
abandoned in Egypt was finally replaced by the new one in
Canaan. Egypt was marked by the handiwork of man, 'a garden
of vegetables', all carefully planned and laid out. Canaan, on
the other hand, displayed the handiwork of God, for it was 'a
land of hills and valleys'. Everywhere the eye was refreshed and
delighted by the unorganised order of the great Creator.

Egypt's fertility, as dependent on water as Canaan's, was
irrigated by the foot. I noticed that this was still in use when I
was in Egypt in the Second World War. A simple device,
worked by the foot, pumps the water from the Nile so that it
flows to where it is needed. It is a supply dependent on human
ingenuity and energy.

How different it was with Canaan, a land 'which drinks
water by the rain from heaven'. This new country that God had
prepared for His people was made fruitful by that which came
down from above. That Canaan should be completely dependent on the heavens for water was God's idea. If the
heavens were shut up, then something must be wrong.[8] The
spiritual reason must be sought out and the matter speedily
rectified. There was no escaping the issue by devising an
alternative supply.

In Canaan if the rain doesn't come, you either get right or get
out! All too often God's people have preferred to opt out. They
have abandoned Canaan for Egypt. Stephen, in his great de-
fence, reminds us how Israel, after they had been delivered
from Egypt through Moses, refused to obey him, and 'in their
hearts they turned to Egypt'.[9] These things are intended to be a
warning to us. How often in its long and chequered history the
church has failed to heed the voice of Him who uses brazen

heavens to speak. Instead it has turned to the substitutes of
Egypt, preferring the working of the foot to the bowing of the
knee. 'Woe to those who go down to Egypt for help . . . but do
not look to the Holy One of Israel or consult the Lord!'[10]
Because revival comes from heaven it provides a powerful cor-
rective to worldly methods. No one bothers with the pump
when rain is deluging the land.

Revival is recognised as clearly 'heaven-sent', when men
cannot account for what is happening in terms of human personality or organisation, and when the work continues unabated
without human control. When a movement becomes organised
or controlled by man, it has ceased to be spontaneous – it is no
longer revival. The course of the 1904 Welsh Revival has been
outlined thus:

> God commenced to work.
> Then the devil began to work in opposition.
> Then God worked all the harder.
> Finally man began to work, and the revival came to an end.

It is of course necessary that leaders ensure that the work of
the Spirit is not infiltrated by false doctrine or practice, but
great care needs to be taken that we do not take things out of
the control of the Holy Spirit. When God has put His hand on
the helm we do well to keep ours off.

NOTES

1. Acts 2:2
2. Ps. 64:7, 9
3. 2 Chron. 29:36
4. Acts 2:6, 7
5. Isa. 42:9
6. Acts 3:19
7. Deut. 11:10, 11
8. Deut. 11:16, 17
9. Acts 7:39
10. Isa. 31:1

7. GOD-CONSCIOUSNESS

In imagination take your place with the hundred and twenty on that historic day of Pentecost. Suddenly the voice of prayer is stilled as every ear catches high up in the heavens a sound that resembles an approaching hurricane. Nearer and nearer it comes, until it seems to fill the very house where you are sitting. At that very moment you see supernatural fire, dividing into tongues of flame and alighting on you, and those around you. How would you feel? Well, that was doubtless how the disciples felt! They were over-awed by the presence of God. Here we touch the heart of our subject, for the spirit of revival is the consciousness of God.

As a light from heaven, brighter than the noonday sun, struck Saul of Tarsus to the ground, and brought him, convicted and broken, to the feet of Christ, so does the Eternal Light in days of revival burst upon the slumbering consciousness of men. At Pentecost God manifested His presence first to His disciples – that's where revival always begins – then to the assembled multitude through the preaching of Peter, so that 'they were cut to the heart',[1] until at length the mysterious influence from heaven had spread across the city, 'and fear came upon every soul'.[2]

'He will baptise you in holy spirit and fire'[3] (to give a literal rendering) is how John the Baptiser predicted this Pentecostal experience. If here we translate the Greek word for 'spirit' by its secondary meaning of 'wind' (as in John 3:8, 'the wind blows . . .'), John is promising that Jesus would baptise them in the twin elements of 'holy wind and fire'. This is exactly what happened on the day of Pentecost. Wind symbolises God's limitless power, fire His purity. In times of revival God comes in wind and fire.

Pentecost was intensely personal. The wind bore down upon the disciples, filling the house where they were. The tongues of fire sat upon each of them. It was more than God manifesting His power and purity to men, He was coming upon *them* to make them powerful and pure. Significantly, it was in the semblance of a dove that the Spirit had come upon the sinless Son. But now God is dealing with His imperfect followers. Though they had prepared themselves in those ten days of waiting, they still needed the purging flame.

Men are only made conscious of God by the display of His attributes. They feel God when they sense His greatness, His love, or His wisdom. But in times of revival it is especially His power and His holiness that are in evidence. It is these that bring that deep conviction of sin among believing and unbelieving alike. In times of revival a man is not only made conscious that God is there, but often it will seem to him that He is there to deal with him alone. He becomes oblivious of everyone but himself in the agonising grip of a holy God.

The ruthless logic of Jonathan Edward's famous sermon, 'Sinners in the hands of an angry God', preached in his usual undemonstrative manner during the New England revival of 1741, could never have produced the effect it did, had it not been for the consciousness of God that gripped the hearers. 'When they went into the meeting-house,' wrote Trumbull, 'the appearance of the assembly was thoughtless and vain; the people scarcely conducted themselves with common decency.' But when it came to the sermon, 'the assembly appeared bowed with an awful conviction of their sin and danger. There was such a breathing of distress and weeping, that the preacher was obliged to speak to the people and desire silence that he might be heard.'

Similar is the scene described by Charles Finney, when he preached in the village schoolhouse near Antwerp, N.Y.: 'An awful solemnity seemed to settle upon the people; the congregation began to fall from their seats in every direction and cry for mercy. If I had had a sword in each hand I could not have cut them down as fast as they fell. I was obliged to stop preaching.' Though the measure of the Spirit's conviction will vary from occasion to occasion, and even from person to person, the explanation is always the same, the manifestation of God in holiness and power.

At times this strange sense of God may pervade a building, a community or a district, affecting those who come within its spell. In the Welsh Revival of 1904 near the town of Gorseinon a meeting continued throughout the night. A miner, a hardened godless character, returning from his shift about four a.m., saw the light in the chapel and decided to investigate. As soon as he opened the door he was overwhelmed by a sense of God's presence. He was heard to exclaim, 'Oh, God is here!' He was afraid either to enter or depart, and there on the threshold of the chapel the work of salvation began in his heart.

No town in Ulster was more deeply affected by the 1859 Revival than Coleraine. A boy at school was so troubled about his spiritual condition that he had to be sent home. An older boy, who was a Christian, accompanied him and before they had gone far led him to Christ. Returning at once to the school this latest convert testified to the schoolmaster, 'Oh, I am so happy! I have the Lord Jesus in my heart.' The effect of these artless words was extraordinary. Boy after boy rose and silently left the room. When the master investigated what was happening to his class he found these boys ranged alongside the wall of the playground, everyone apart and on his knees! Their silent prayer soon became a bitter cry which brought conviction to those inside – not only the other boys, but to the girls' schoolroom above. Soon the whole school was on its knees, and its wail of distress brought people flocking in from the street who, as they crossed the threshold, came under the same convicting power. Every room was filled with men, women and children seeking God.

In the great American Revival of 1858, ships, as they drew near the American ports, seemed to come into a zone of the Spirit's influence. Ship after ship arrived with the same tale of sudden conviction and conversion. In one ship a captain and the entire crew of thirty men found Christ out at sea and entered the harbour rejoicing.

This sense of God bringing conviction of sin in its wake, is perhaps the outstanding feature of true revival. Not always is it the unconverted who are affected, as in the cases just quoted. Often it is believers, or those who profess to be, as in the revivals in Manchuria and China under Jonathan Goforth (1906–9), or in the more recent Congo Revival (1953). Describing the revival in Northampton, Mass. (1735), Jonathan Edwards wrote, 'The town seemed to be full of the presence of God. It never was so full of love, nor so full of joy, and yet so full of distress, as it was then.' To cleansed hearts it is heaven, to convicted hearts hell, when God is in the midst.

NOTES

1. Acts 2:37
2. Acts 2:43
3. Luke 3:16 Lit. Trans.

8. FILLED VESSELS

Still looking at Pentecost as a model outpouring of the Holy Spirit, we come to the statement, 'They were all filled with the Holy Spirit'. Up to this point no outsiders have been involved, only the one hundred and twenty disciples. This is a principle of God's ways in revival. He does not begin by regenerating the outsider but by reviving the 'insider'. 'Wilt Thou not revive *us* again, that *Thy people* may rejoice in Thee?'[1] It is always God's plan first to renew His people, and then through them to reach the world.

This experience of being filled with the Spirit is an indispensable element in any true visitation. The question is often asked, 'Is the filling with the Holy Spirit of a number of believers revival?' Not necessarily. You cannot have revival, in the sense in which we use the word here, without believers being filled with the Spirit, but the fact that believers are filled does not of itself constitute revival or result in revival. In this chapter we are touching one important ingredient, but there must be others before we are justified in asserting, 'This is it!'

Many speak of the current charismatic movement as revival. There are instances of the charismatic movement sparking off revival, or of revivals breaking out which manifest charismatic features, but it is a mistake to identify revival with the charismatic movement as a whole. There may be evidence of believers entering into a genuine experience of the power and gifts of the Spirit, without the other hallmarks of revival being apparent. At such times there is *reviving* but not *revival*. For the Spirit to come upon believers, for them to speak in tongues and exercise other spiritual gifts, were all part of normal New Testament experience; but for the Holy Spirit so to work in and through the church that the community was powerfully affected – that was a thing of special times and seasons. This is clear from the Acts record.

Although many are filled with the Spirit in revival, we do not need to wait for such a powerful visitation to be filled. Two significant facts emerge from a careful examination of the New Testament as a whole, and it is important that we give due weight to every section of it, the historical as well as the doctrinal. The view that we must draw our doctrine from the teaching portions (the epistles), but not the narrative portions (the gospels and the Acts) implies that these two sections of the New Testament are at variance. Apart from this, it is contrary to Paul's assertion that 'all Scripture is . . . profitable for doctrine'.[2]

The first fact that is clear from the teaching of the gospels and the history of the Acts is that the Holy Spirit never identifies or confuses this powerful encounter with the Holy Spirit, about which we are speaking, with the initial regenerating work of the Spirit usually called conversion. In other words, because I am a child of God through repentance and faith does not mean that I have been immersed in the Holy Spirit and fire. Dealing with the oft-heard assertion, 'We got it all at conversion', a well-known preacher retorted, 'Got it all! Got it all! Then in heaven's name, where is it?'

The second fact that we glean from the epistles is that the New Testament writers always assume that those to whom they wrote, however young and immature in the faith, had had this encounter. They remind the believers of how they had received the Spirit,[3] been sealed with the Spirit,[4] been baptised in the

Spirit,[5] experienced a rich outpouring of the Spirit[6] – terms which those who assume that we get it automatically at conversion seldom if ever use. These terms only become meaningful when we link them with a clearly identifiable experience. Nowhere are the young New Testament churches exhorted to pray for or receive the Holy Spirit. 'Be filled with the Spirit'[7] means 'Go on being filled . . .', which implies that they had already experienced an initial filling. It does not tell believers to *obtain*, but simply to *maintain* this blessing.

It may be objected, that if the New Testament writers always assume that those to whom they wrote had received the Holy Spirit, does not that prove that this experience must have been part of their new birth experience? It is helpful here to compare Spirit baptism with water baptism and, in any case, these two events are closely connected in the Acts record.[8] Why do we never find in the epistles an exhortation to be baptised in water? Because the writers always assume that it has taken place.[9] But this does not mean that the new birth and water baptism are identical. Just as it is possible to be born again without being baptised in water, so it is equally possible to be born again without being baptised in the Spirit.

It is a tragic mistake to assume that this experience has taken place in the life of every believer, unless there is clear evidence of it. When Paul came across a group of disciples who evidently lacked the hallmarks of the Spirit's presence and power, we find him dealing with them over water baptism, rather than the new birth, and then laying his hands upon them for the Holy Spirit.[10] In New Testament times the experience clearly belonged to the beginning of the Christian life: new birth, water baptism, and then the coming upon of the Spirit was the usual but not invariable order. Like water baptism, it was intended to be part of Christian initiation, and becomes so today whenever it is taught to converts as it was in New Testament times. Like water baptism, it is a crisis of obedience and faith, not a process of sanctification. Nor is there any question of having to wait till we are knowledgeable enough, sanctified enough, or mature enough before we can receive our inheritance in the Holy Spirit. As Peter said at the first outpouring, 'For the promise is to you and to your children and to all that are far off, every one whom the Lord our God calls to Him.'[11] But remember, like most promises in the Bible, we must fulfil the appropriate conditions and stake our claim.

'They were *all* filled with the Spirit.' It would seem that God was determined to emphasise from the outset that He intended this to be a universal experience for His people, not just for the select few as was the case under the Old Covenant. Those disciples of the upper room[12] must have presented an interesting cross-section of the fruit of our Lord's earthly ministry. There were 'the Twelve', Mary and the other womenfolk, the brothers of Jesus who did not believe in Him when we last read about them,[13] and the rest. Some older, some younger. Some educated, some unlearned. Some seasoned and others newly converted. But significantly, 'they were *all* filled', not just 'the Twelve' and those with a leading rôle. God's terms of reference have not altered. It is still for *all*.

'They were all *filled* with the Holy Spirit.' Right here we have the secret of the astonishing 'success story' of those first Christians. Such power from heaven was released in Jerusalem, that, like a great boulder dropped into a pond, it was to set in motion waves of blessing which would ultimately break on earth's farthest shores. Not only have revivals been times when large numbers have been filled with the Spirit, but the filling has often, as here at Pentecost, sparked things off.

During the revivals that blessed America in the last century, four Christian sailors on the American battleship *North Carolina* began to meet for prayer in the bowels of the ship. One evening they were filled with the Spirit and burst into song. Ungodly shipmates, who came down to mock, stayed to pray.

The laugh of the scornful became the cry of the penitent. A glorious work broke out that continued night after night until it became necessary to send ashore for ministers to help, and the battleship became a Bethel.

One morning in 1821, a young lawyer from the town of Adams, New York state, was converted as he prayed to God out in the woods. That evening Charles Finney experienced a powerful baptism in the Spirit and next day, through his instrumentality, revival broke out in the town, and in due course spread through all that region of America. Speaking of the relationship between the baptism in the Spirit and revival, Finney once said:

> Many times great numbers of persons in a community will be clothed with this power, when the very atmosphere of the whole place seems to be charged with the life of God. Strangers coming into it and passing through the place will be instantly smitten with conviction of sin, and in many instances converted to Christ.

As far as the outbreak of revival is concerned you may have to pray and wait, but you do not need to wait for the filling of the Spirit. The risen Lord is longing to bestow. It is part of the salvation He died to win. It is something you are to claim as your heavenly birthright. To be filled is to be God-possessed. Stretch out your hands to God; only make sure they are *clean hands* for this is a condition of receiving any blessing from Him.[14] They should also be *empty hands*, as they were when you reached out for salvation, for you cannot earn or merit what you seek as a gift. Like eternal life, it is a 'charisma' or gift of grace. They must also be *longing hands*, for 'thirst' is a vital condition of receiving.[15] If you desire with all your heart you will surely receive. Finally they must be *believing hands* – not held out plaintively and passively in the hope that God *may* give sometime, if I'm lucky; – but hands that reach out with strong confidence, that grasp the promise and will not let go until heaven has answered.

NOTES

1. Ps. 85:6
2. Tim. 3:16 AV
3. Gal. 3:2
4. Eph. 1:13
5. 1 Cor. 12:13
6. Titus 3:6
7. Eph. 5:18
8. Acts 10:47, etc.
9. 1 Cor. 1:14–15
10. Acts 19:5–6
11. Acts 2:39
12. Acts 1:13–14
13. John 7:5
14. Ps. 24:4–5
15. John 7:37–39

9. SIGNS AND WONDERS

A sign or wonder is necessarily something which is done out in the open for all to see. When the disciples began to speak in other tongues, the sound evidently drew the multitude together to witness what was taking place. 'Thus, tongues are a sign not for believers but for unbelievers.'[1] Of course, Paul nowhere insists that this is the only purpose of tongues or even the main purpose. Earlier in the same chapter he had made it clear that the gift of tongues had a personal ministry of edification to the individual who exercised it, as well as a public ministry of edification to the church when accompanied by interpretation.[2] On the day of Pentecost, however, tongues became a sign that caused the multitudes to wonder.

Signs and wonders are a characteristic of revival, as the histories of revivals abundantly confirm. Peter's Pentecost sermon confirms this, for he reminds us that the outpouring of the Spirit, according to Joel's prophecy, would be accompanied by 'wonders in the heaven above and signs on the earth beneath'.[3] Like many other Christians, I had been dutifully taught that signs and wonders, together with the spiritual gifts of 1 Corinthians 12, passed away with the apostolic age. I never found the supporting arguments very convincing, but it was a study of revival that for me finally nailed the coffin of this theory.

As I read of dreams and visions, tongues and interpretations, revelations and trances, prophesyings and healings, tremblings and prostrations, and numerous other wonders that I had never personally witnessed and were not part of the Christian scene as I and my fellow Christians knew it, I began to see that what I had been taught was contradicted by facts too numerous and powerful to be disregarded. I began to suspect that the view that God had withdrawn these gifts and that signs and wonders had now ceased was a theory of convenience – a cover-up for the real reasons why we no longer had them.

The God of the Old Testament revealed Himself as, 'majestic in holiness, terrible in glorious deeds, doing wonders'.[4] It never seemed to have occurred to those naive New Testament believers that He might have changed. They were evidently 'at home' in the supernatural. The first recorded prayer of the early church was that God would stretch out His hand to heal, and that signs and wonders would be performed through the name of Jesus.[5]

In all the teaching of 1 Corinthians 12–14, regulating the use of gifts in the church, I could find no hint that these were only to last for the few decades of the apostolic era, and that all this inspired teaching would soon become, for all practical purposes, obsolete. It is true that Chapter 13 speaks of prophecy, tongues and (word of) knowledge passing away; but this would be, as the passage goes on to show, 'when the perfect comes'; that is, when we no longer see, as now, in a mirror dimly, but 'face to face'; and when we no longer know in part but fully, even as we have been known.[6] In other words, at the return of Christ.

The writings of the sub-apostolic era do not bear out the assertion that the supernatural manifestations of New Testament times suddenly ceased at the close of the first century. It is a matter of historical fact that they continued, although decreasing in frequency, far into the succeeding centuries. In his *History of the Apostolic Church* Philip Schaff writes:

The speaking with tongues, however, was not confined to the day of Pentecost; together with the other extraordinary spiritual gifts ... this gift also perpetuated itself in the church. We find traces of it still in the second and third centuries.[7]

Herbert Workman provides further proof in his *Persecution in the Early Church*:

St. Augustine, whom no one can accuse of either insincerity or stupidity, solemnly asserts that in his own diocese of Hippo, in the space of two years, there had occurred no less than seventy-two miracles, among them five cases of restoration to life.[8]

Horace Bushnell, well-known American preacher and theologian of the last century, carefully investigated the view that the miraculous gifts were to cease, and called it 'a clumsy assumption'. He wrote, 'That there never has been a formal discontinuance I am perfectly satisfied. I know no proof to the contrary that appears to me to have a straw's weight.'[9]

There is no disputing that the gifts lapsed to a great extent in the centuries that followed the apostolic age. But there is an explanation of this that accords much more with the facts than the theory that God withdrew them because the church, now in possession of a complete Bible, no longer needed them. Revivals have always had the tendency to restore the church to apostolic Christianity – to effect a recovery however temporary, of the spirit and power of the first century. 'The apostolical times seem to have returned upon us,' wrote an eyewitness of the eighteenth century revival in New England. God tends to manifest His power in these supernatural ways through a revived church, but to withdraw that power when the church is in spiritual decline. This would mean that the lapsing of the gifts in those early centuries has far more to do with the decline of 'the body' than with the design of 'the Head'. This is disturbing. We can no longer explain the dearth of the mighty works of God by a simple appeal to the sovereign will of God. We have to ask ourselves, 'To what extent does the responsibility lie at our door?'

It is heartening to find in such a conservative work as *The Devotional Commentary* this balanced statement about spiritual gifts, commenting on the verse, 'Do not quench the Spirit':[10]

> In times of spiritual blessing these gifts [of inspired utterance] are more especially manifest. It has been so in every great revival from the days of Wesley and Whitfield to the days of Evan Roberts. Such gifts, coming indeed from the Spirit, are not to be quenched, put out, like a lamp no longer needed or a fire that meant danger. Nor must such utterance – 'prophesyings' not necessarily predictive, but claiming to be of divine impulse – be despised. They are indeed commended by St. Paul.[11] They are to be received with respect and yet with intelligent discrimination.

No one should conclude from what I have said that these manifestations of the Spirit are confined to times of revival. This was certainly not the case in New Testament times, for they were looked upon as one important aspect of the normal functioning of the church. But down the centuries, when these gifts have been conspicuous by their absence, God has used revival to throw them up, as if to say, 'Look! I haven't changed. I am still able and willing to work as in Bible times if My people will dare to open their hearts to me and believe.' So often, even amongst deeply devoted Christians, hearts are shut by fear.

Some readers may have the mistaken impression that all

such manifestations in modern times have been confined to the Pentecostal movement of the turn of the century, or the more recent charismatic movement in the churches. I want therefore to illustrate what I have been saying from the account of a revival in South India over one hundred years ago, long before the modern Pentecostal movement.

In 1860 revival broke out in Tinevelly, South India. The man whom God used in the movement was a national evangelist called Aroolappen, and the movement began ('Tell it not in Gath!') in the Brethren assemblies in which A. N. Groves, one of the early Brethren leaders, had laboured. Aroolappen described the beginning of the movement:

> From the 4th May to the 7th the Holy Spirit was poured out openly and wonderfully. Some prophesied and rebuked the people: some beat themselves on their breasts severely, and trembled and fell down through the shaking of their bodies and souls ... They saw some signs in the air. They were much pleased to praise God. Some ignorant (i.e. uninstructed) people gave out some songs and hymns that we never heard before ... All the heathen marvelled, and came and saw and heard us with fearful minds ...
>
> In the month of June some of our people praised the Lord by unknown tongues, with their interpretations. In the month of July the Spirit was poured out upon our congregation at Oleikollam, and above twenty-five persons were baptised. They are steadfast in prayers ... Some missionaries admit the truth of the gifts of the Holy Spirit. The Lord meets everywhere one after another, though some tried to quench the Spirit.

Henry Groves, a son of A.N. Groves, writing in the *Indian Watchman* for July 1860, takes up the story:

> The spirit of prophecy was given to some there, and a little

boy said that in a certain village which he named, about a mile distant, the Spirit of God had been poured out. Within a quarter of an hour some men and women came from that village beating their breasts in great fear and alarm of conscience. They fell down and rolled on the ground. This continued a short time. They all asked to have prayer made for them after which they said with great joy, 'The Lord Jesus has forgiven our sins', and clapping their hands together in the fulness of their hearts' gladness, they embraced one another.

For nearly three days this ecstatic joy appears to have lasted. They ate nothing except a little food taken in the evening, and passing sleepless nights they continued the whole time in reading of the word, in prayer and in singing praises to the Lord. Of some it is said, 'they lifted up their eyes to heaven and saw blood and fire and pillars of smoke, and speaking loud they told what they had seen.'[12]

Several missionaries, at first sceptical or even opposed to the movement, were won over when they saw the fruit of it, and were compelled to admit that the work was of God, though some remained dubious of the revival phenomena. The depth and permanence of the Spirit's work was self-evident. Of those really influenced, there appeared to be not one case of a convert falling back.

In New Testament times God used signs to authenticate the truth of the gospel. Said Nicodemus to Jesus, 'We know that you are a teacher come from God; for no one can do these signs that you do, unless God is with him.'[13] After Christ's ascension His disciples 'went forth and preached everywhere, while the Lord worked with them and *confirmed the message by the signs that attended it*.'[14] Hebrews reminds us that God bore witness to the apostolic preaching 'by signs and wonders and various miracles and by gifts of the Holy Spirit distributed according to His own will'.[15] Significantly, every powerful movement of the Spirit recorded in the Acts, which resulted in large numbers turning to Christ, was characterised by some sign or wonder that touched people's hearts and prepared them for the gospel.

At a time of growing materialism and scepticism, how greatly we need this kind of divine authentication. When we dare to present to them a God who not only answers by preaching but by fire, they will respond to us as they did to Elijah, 'It is well spoken'.[16] Logically enough they believe that if our God is the God of the Bible He must be supernatural. Otherwise he is mythical. May God purge our hearts of unbelief that He may take the veil from the nation's eyes.

NOTES

1. 1 Cor. 14:22
2. 1 Cor. 14:4, 26–27
3. Acts 2:19
4. Exod. 15:11
5. Acts 4:30
6. 1 Cor. 13:8–12
7. Book 1. Sec. 55
8. Wyvern Books Series. p. 61
9. From *Nature and the Supernatural* chap. 14
10. 1 Thes. 5:19
11. 1 Cor. 14:1, 39
12. *The History and Diaries of an Indian Christian* by G. H. Long
13. John 3:2
14. Matt. 16:20
15. Heb. 2:4
16. 1 Kings 18:24

10. DIVINE MAGNETISM

Ezekiel records how he prophesied in vision to the dry bones that were scattered over the valley, and 'there was a noise ... and the bones came together'.[1] Similarly at Pentecost there was a divine magnetism at work, for we read, 'at this sound the multitude came together'.[2] On this occasion it was the speaking in tongues that was the magnetic agent. Though God will often in times of revival use a manifestation of the Spirit in this way, this strange drawing may occur when there is no such outward sign or wonder.

We see this in the powerful movement of the Spirit associated with the ministry of John the Baptist. John did no miracle,[3] but his ministry was one continuous miracle, for he emptied the city of Jerusalem, all Judea, and the region around the Jordan, as the people flocked to his baptism.[4] What drew them? Christ Himself put the question to the crowds. Was it to see a reed trembling in the wind? John was the very antithesis of that: a sterling character who called the religious leaders 'a brood of vipers' and even rebuked the king on the throne for his immorality. Was it to see a man dressed in silks and satins? Imagine the ripple of laughter that swept through the crowd as they thought of John in his Elijah-like garb of hair-shirt and leather belt! No, it was to see one who was a prophet – and more than a prophet, one anointed of God to prepare the way of the

Messiah.[5] There was no explaining the drawing power of John apart from the magnetism of the Spirit.

This same feature was apparent all through our Lord's earthly ministry. There is no more remarkable case than that of the Gadarene demoniac. One might have imagined that when Jesus turned up, this demon-driven man would have headed off in the opposite direction. Instead, he ran to meet Jesus and worshipped Him,[6] and Jesus responded by setting him free. See it again in the ministry of the apostles. Paul and Barnabas preached in the synagogue in Antioch-in-Pisidia, but we do not read of any healing or other phenomenon taking place. Yet 'the next sabbath almost the whole city gathered together to hear the word of God'.[7]

During the early days of the Lewis Awakening (1949) there was a powerful movement in the village of Arnol. There had been no response during the first few meetings, and a time of prayer had been convened in a home at the close of an evening meeting. There was a moment when all became aware that prayer had been heard, and that God's Spirit was being poured out on the village. As they went outside, they found that the people were all leaving their cottages and making their way, as though drawn by some unseen force, to one point in the village. There they assembled and waited. When Duncan Campbell began to preach, the word took immediate effect. In a few days that small village community had been powerfully affected, the drinking house was closed, and many had been converted to Christ.

The modern evangelist is faced with two major problems. The first is how to draw people from their homes, their firesides, their television sets to hear his message. And the second is how to bring them to repentance and faith. Obviously the first is only a means to the second, but the second cannot be achieved without the first. We may reflect ruefully that Paul didn't have to contend with television addicts. The fact is that we do, and spiritual gimmicks do not provide an answer. How futile it is to expect the man of the world to forsake his 'thing' because we offer him our 'thing'. At this level it is impossible to compete with the world, nor does God intend us to try. He has a better way.

It should be a matter of concern that the church's outreach today is only touching a small proportion of the community. That some are being converted should not obscure the fact that the masses are largely unreached. And those who are converted are mostly people with church connections or who have some contact with Christian friends. With what energy and imagination organising committees will strive to alter this situation! Large sums spent on publicity, witness marches through the streets, and the meetings not lacking in items and features to provide variety and interest. The fact that all this did not really accomplish the desired end last time is only ground for trying it all again with greater energy and imagination. The high proportion of 'drop-outs' amongst those professing conversion must be rectified by a more thorough training of counsellors, and greater care in follow-up. And so it goes on.

It required no outpouring of the Spirit to bring Simon Peter to Jesus, only the invitation of Andrew. We certainly have our part to play in bringing people to Christ. But where normal means are failing it is no use adopting the extra-special means; it is the supernatural to which we must turn. On Carmel there was no response to Elijah's fervent pleading, but the moment God answered by fire the people were on their faces. What the efforts and ingenuity of man cannot accomplish is but the work of a moment to the outpoured Spirit. You may be sure that when God works the people will be there, drawn not by human persuasion, but by the magnetism of heaven.

There are times when God calls us to cease from our own endeavours so as to enlist His powerful intervention. It is possible that *our* activity may be the major blockage to *His*

Rain from Heaven

activity. 'But can God not work in spite of us?' we may ask. Certainly, but the fact is He has chosen to work *through* us, and our sincere efforts may be hindering Him from doing just that. At such times we are brought to acknowledge with Jehoshaphat, 'We are powerless against this great multitude ... but our eyes are upon Thee.' Then we may expect the answer, 'The battle is not yours but God's ... You will not need to fight in this battle; take your position, stand still, and see the victory of the Lord on your behalf.'[8]

NOTES

1. Ezek. 37:7
2. Acts 2:6
3. John 10:41
4. Matt. 3:5
5. Matt 11:7–9
6. Mark 5:6
7. Acts 13:44
8. 2 Chron. 20:12, 17

11. PROPHETIC PREACHING

Having been drawn by the magnetism of the Spirit, the crowds at Pentecost were then exposed to the preaching of the good news. 'Peter, standing with the eleven, lifted up his voice and addressed them.'[1] Had we been there listening to Peter's message I think we should have detected that here was something very different from the gospel sermons we hear today. In its spirit and form it would have taken us back to the Old Testament prophet, rather than forward to the modern gospel preacher. In fact, we could sum up the distinctiveness of this kind of preaching in a word: it was 'prophetic'.

Those who do not find room in their thinking for the operation of spiritual gifts, are usually quick to point out that New Testament 'prophesying' is not necessarily predictive. This of course is quite true. But when they go on to imply that nothing more than preaching is intended they are failing to see that basically prophecy is *inspired utterance*. Paul makes it abundantly clear that prophecy, teaching and exhortation are 'gifts that differ'.[2] We are missing something important when we try to make them the same.

Some are afraid to accept the validity of prophetic utterance today because, in their view, that would be to put such utterance on a par with inspired Scripture – to add in fact to the Word of God. This is based on a misunderstanding. The canon of Holy Scripture is of course complete; by it every other utterance must be judged. But this does not mean that all inspired utterance has now come to an end. What about the discourses of Jesus that Scripture has not recorded? Were they any less inspired by the Holy Spirit because God did not see fit to enshrine them in Holy Writ? When the Spirit came upon the twelve disciples at Ephesus they 'prophesied'.[3] Philip the evangelist had four daughters who 'prophesied'.[4] There were many others in the churches who also prophesied. Though their utterances have not been recorded in Scripture they were none the less inspired by the Spirit. Only a very small proportion of what the Spirit has inspired was needed for the written record of God's revealed truth. The rest was simply for immediate use and application.

I am not insisting that Peter was actually prophesying in his great Pentecost sermon, but that there was a distinct prophetic or inspirational element in his preaching. It was as spontaneous as the outpouring that produced it. There is no evidence that God gave him three days' notice that he had to deliver a sermon to convince several thousand of his fellow countrymen that Jesus was the Messiah. His heart had been deeply prepared by ten days of prayer, and when the moment came, anointed with fresh oil, God filled his mouth with words. 'For what you are to say will be given to you in that hour,' Jesus had promised them, 'for it is not you who speak, but the Spirit of your Father speaking through you.'[5] Though Jesus had been referring primarily to times when His disciples would stand on trial before kings and governors, the promise was evidently to have wider fulfilment in the seizing of many unexpected opportunities to preach Christ. Allowing that there is a place for the deliberate and carefully prepared presentation of the gospel, we must not lose sight of the inspirational and unpremeditated preaching which is so characteristic when the Spirit is working in power. It is a distinct feature of revival.

Another characteristic of prophetic preaching is its *rel-*

evance to the immediate situation of the hearers. The message of the Old Testament prophet might contain predictive elements that would span the centuries to come, but primarily he spoke directly to the condition and situation of his hearers. As A. W. Tozer points out, to stand in the pulpit and declare that twice two is four may be true, but it is hardly relevant! How much preaching today provides convincing answers to questions no one is asking! It is true but irrelevant. How dexterously Peter related the things that God had spoken by the prophets to the immediate situation, so that the hearers found themselves compelled to identify, until the arrows of conviction had pierced their consciences.

In his autobiography which records the many years of his labours in revival, Charles Finney wrote:

> For some twelve years of my earliest ministry, I wrote not a word; and was commonly obliged to preach without any preparation whatever, except what I got in prayer. Oftentimes I went into the pulpit without knowing upon what text I should speak, or a word that I should say. I depended on the occasion and the Holy Spirit to suggest the text, and to open the whole subject to my mind; and certainly in no part of my ministry have I preached with greater success and power. If I did not preach from inspiration I don't know how I did preach. It was a common experience with me . . . that the subject would open up to my mind in a manner that was surprising to myself. It seemed that I could see with intuitive clearness just what I ought to say, and whole platoons of thoughts, words and illustrations came to me as fast as I could deliver them.

There was a rugged boldness about Peter's preaching that reminds one of the fearless prophets of Old Testament days. Centuries before this Micah had declared, 'I am filled with

power, with the Spirit of the Lord ... to declare to Jacob his
transgression and to Israel his sin.'[6] Clearly Peter had lit his
torch from the same sacred fire as he arraigned his hearers with
the murder of their Messiah.

When a prophet is accepted and deified his message is lost.
The prophet is only useful so long as he is stoned as a public
nuisance calling us to repentance, disturbing our comfortable
routines, breaking our respectable idols, shattering our
sacred conventions (A. G. Gardiner).

Jesus had told the apostles that when the Holy Spirit had
come to them He would 'convince the world of sin',[7] and how
effectively He did just that through Peter's sermon! To aim at
'decisions' or 'results' before this work of convincing has been
done is to build one's castle on the sand. What is the good of
offering a man a pardon when he has never been convicted of
the crime? What is the good of urging a man to come to Jesus
when he has no sense of his 'lostness'? Revival preaching has
always been preaching with 'A grasp on the conscience'. It was
said of Gilbert Tennent, a preacher of the New England
Revival:

He seemed to ... aim directly at the hearts and consciences
of his hearers, to lay open their ruinous delusions, show them
their numerous, secret, hypocritical shifts in religion, and
drive them out of every deceitful refuge wherein they made
themselves easy with the form of godliness without the
power. [8]

At the end of Peter's sermon there was 'an appeal', only it
did not come from the preacher but from the congregation:
'Brethren, what shall we do?' So deeply were they convicted of
their sin that they were desperate for pardon and peace.

'Repent, and be baptised . . .', responded the preacher. As with
the preaching of John the Baptist, Our Lord himself, and then
His apostles, 'Repent' was the clarion call. God 'commands all
men everywhere to repent', and especially in times of revival
the Spirit of God takes up the cry through the lips of anointed
messengers, and the valley of decision is thronged with multitudes pressing through to true commitment.

This kind of Spirit-inspired preaching, bringing conviction
in its train, is well illustrated by Charles Finney's description
of how revival broke out in a settlement called Evan Mills:

> I had not taken a thought with regard to what I should
> preach. The Holy Spirit was upon me, and I felt confident
> that when the time came for action I should know. As soon
> as I found the house packed I arose and, without any formal
> introduction of singing, opened upon them with these words:
> 'Say to the righteous that it shall be well with him; for they
> shall eat the fruit of their doings. Woe to the wicked! It shall
> be ill with him; for the reward of his hands shall be given
> him.'
>
>   The Spirit of God came upon me with such power that it
> was like opening a battery upon them. For more than an hour
> the word of God came through me to them in a manner that I
> could see was carrying all before it. It was a fire and a
> hammer breaking the rock, and as the sword that was pierc-
> ing . . . I saw that a general conviction was spreading over
> the whole congregation.

The one simple explanation of the effects of revival preaching is the power of the Holy Spirit resting upon the preacher.
Peter had been newly filled. His preaching was the overflow. A
man may not possess great gifts of eloquence, but if he has this
anointing his ministry will be effective. It was said of Savona-
rola, the Italian reformer, that 'nature had withheld from him

almost all the gifts of the orator'. Yet his biographer speaks of

> his unconquerable persistance in seeking the power of the
> Highest, till his thoughts and affections were so absorbed in
> God by the power of the Holy Spirit, that ... we are not
> amazed at the character and effects of his preaching – so
> pathetic, so melting, so resistless that the reporter lays down
> his pen with this apology written under the last line – 'Such
> sorrow and weeping came upon me that I could go no
> further'.

Prophetic preaching is first and last preaching 'through the
Holy Spirit sent from heaven'.[10] The revival preacher is the
man who can say with his Master, 'The Spirit of the Lord is
upon me, because He has anointed me'.

NOTES

1. Acts 2:14
2. Rom. 12:6–8
3. Acts 19:6
4. Acts 21:9
5. Matt. 10:19–20
6. Mic. 3:8
7. John 16:8
8. *Christian History* (*1743–4*) by Thos Prince
9. Acts 17:30
10. 1 Pet. 1:12

12. THE OVERFLOW

There have been many distinctive movements of the Spirit that have blessed the church, but which one would hesitate to call 'revival' because of the absence of this essential feature: overflow to the community at large. This has been largely true of the present day charismatic movement. The church may have been deeply affected but there was no effect on the world. If the man in the street has to scrutinise a religious paper to discover that 'revival' is on, we may well pause and ask, 'Is this the real thing?' God's people are called to be 'the salt of the earth' and 'the light of the world'. How can He visit them and revive them with an inflow of His power and glory, and the world not know?

That visitation on the day of Pentecost must have seemed to the religious community in Jerusalem like a spiritual bomb. It set off a succession of 'earth tremors' that shook Judaism to its foundations. Let Luke's unvarnished account of the spiritual overflow speak for itself.

So those who received his word were baptised, and there were added that day about three thousand souls.[1]

And the Lord added to their number day by day those who were being saved.[2]

But many of those who heard the word believed; and the number of the men came to about five thousand.[3]

And more than ever believers were added to the Lord, multitudes both of men and women.[4]

And the number of disciples multiplied greatly in Jerusalem,
and a great many of the priests were obedient to the faith.[5]

And all this was within the confines of the city of Jerusalem.
God never intended that this feature of Pentecost should be
unique. Revivals have been characteristically times when God
fulfilled the promise to open the windows of heaven and pour
down such a blessing that there would not be room enough to
receive it.[6] A cursory glance at the histories of these outpourings, even down to this present time, prove that this has
been the case. An eye-witness of the New England Revival of
the eighteenth century wrote:

The dispensation of grace we are now under is . . . in some
circumstances so wonderful, that I believe there has not been
the like since the extraordinary pouring out of the Spirit
immediately after our Lord's ascension.

Many have so described the revivals of their day. In terms of
converts, some of them exceeded even the results of Pentecost.

Of the revivals that took place in America under the preaching of George Whitfield it is estimated that 30,000 were converted to Christ. A century later Dr. Henry Ward Beecher
remarked to Charles Finney concerning the revival that broke
out in 1830, and in which Finney himself was a leading figure,
'This is the greatest revival of religion that has been since the
world began.' It is reckoned that 100,000 were converted that
year in the United States. In the great American revival of
1858, which commenced in the famous Fulton Street prayer
meeting in New York, conversions numbered 50,000 a week,
and over the whole of the United States there could not have

been less than 500,000, according to Finney's computation in 1859 when the movement was still spreading.

Sparks from the American 1858 Revival leapt the watery divide to ignite a similar movement the following year, first in Ulster, and then in every other part of the United Kingdom. Dr. J. Edwin Orr, who has given us the fruits of his detailed research into this movement in his book, *The Second Evangelical Awakening in Britain* (1859) claims that it affected 'every county in Ulster, Scotland, Wales, and England, *adding a millions accessions* to the evangelical churches'. Of course we cannot be certain that 'accessions to ... churches' always spell accessions to the kingdom of God. On the other hand, we do not know how many were truly converted to Christ in non-evangelical churches, or how many conversions were never included in the annual church returns.

More significant than massive statistics is the estimate of the proportion of a community or district vitally affected in these extraordinary times. Conant wrote of the eighteenth-century revival:

It cannot be doubted that at least 50,000 were added to the churches of New England out of a population of 250,000. A fact sufficient to revolutionise, as indeed it did, the religious and moral character, and to determine the destinies of the country.

Many find it hard to believe that there could be in any town or district a wholesale turning of the populace to Christ. God's purpose in this age, they tell us, is not to save the world, but to gather out of the world a people for His name. As a generalisation that is true. Revivals, however, provide us with a number of thrilling examples of what we might call localised and temporary exceptions to this rule. The New Testament itself furnishes us with our first example of this, in connection with the healing through Peter of a cripple called Aeneas. Scripture describes the astonishing result of this miracle by saying, 'All the residents of Lydda and Sharon saw him, and they turned to the Lord.'[7] Jonathan Edwards wrote of the awakening in Northampton, Mass. (1735):

> There was scarcely a single person in the town, either old or young, that was left unconcerned about the great things of the eternal world. Those that were wont to be the vainest and loosest, and those that had been the most disposed to think and speak slightly of vital and experimental religion, were now generally subject to great awakenings. And the work of conversion was carried on in a most astonishing manner, and increased more and more; souls did, as it were, come by flocks to Jesus Christ.

A century later Charles Finney wrote in a similar way of the movement in the town of Rome, New York State: 'As the work proceeded, it gathered in nearly the whole population.'

In 1858, when God was moving so powerfully in the United States, a revival broke out in Sweden. An English minister resident in Stockholm reported, 'I should be disposed to consider that at least 200,000 persons have been awakened out of a population not exceeding 3 millions.' This would mean one out of every fifteen people. Another wrote of the same visitation, 'The awakening is so extensive that there is scarcely a town, a village, or a hamlet, where there is not a little company of believers united together, and edifying one another in love.' Revival inevitably leaves behind such groups, meeting together not because it is the thing to do, but because they have found a new love, a new oneness, a new togetherness in Christ. This leads us to a further mark of revival seen in the outpouring at Pentecost.

NOTES

1. Acts 2:41
2. Acts 2:47
3. Acts 4:4
4. Acts 5:14
5. Acts 6:7
6. Mal. 3:10
7. Acts 9:35

13. COMMUNITY STYLE

In the first ever reference to the church Jesus declared that He himself would build His *'ekklesia'* on a rock foundation, and that the powers of the unseen world would never prevail against it.[1] There was enough dynamite in that simple pronouncement to shatter the thinking of that little band of Jewish disciples. 'But doesn't He mention anything about the renewal of our synagogue worship? Has He not come then to revive our Judaistic faith and renew the primitive worship of our fathers? And what is this "*ekklesia*" He talks of building? Sounds like a new sort of structure – something very different! It's all very disturbing.'

The idea conveyed by *'ekklesia'* was very similar in one respect to that conveyed by 'synagogue', but in another respect very different. Synagogue, from the Greek *sunago* meaning to come together, means a company assembled. *'Ekklesia'* also has the idea of an assembly, but with this important difference. The whole Jewish community could come together to form the synagogue, but the whole community could not form the *ekklesia*, for this word has the special meaning of 'an assembly *called out from* (the community)'. The Greeks used it, as we learn from Acts 19:39, for the select body of responsible citizens who transacted the public affairs of the city, a kind of city council.

Men had to be called out of what they were in to become part of Christ's *'ekklesia'*, and that was where the rub came. It was something Christ was to build from scratch, from its very foundations. So from Pentecost onwards the apostolic message, proclaimed in the power of the Spirit, split the community in two, just as Jesus had predicted.[2] It happened in Pisidian Antioch. 'But the people of the city were divided; some sided with the Jews, and some with the apostles'.[3] Some rejected the message to stay where they were. Others embraced it to find themselves among 'the called out ones', where all racial and social distinctions were obliterated, where they were 'neither Jew nor Greek . . . slave nor free', but 'all one in Christ Jesus'.[4]

From what the Lord was saying it was clear to the disciples that the emergence of this new society would involve conflict – not merely with the religious hierarchy or the representatives of the establishment, but with the powers of the unseen world. But He had made it clear that the final issue was never in doubt. The gates of Hades would not prevail, for by His death and resurrection He would strip Satan of His authority and ensure the final triumph of His church.

We have seen in the Pentecostal outpouring several features that are characteristic of revival. Now we come to the grand objective of the whole operation. It was not merely that a hundred and twenty disciples might be filled, but that they might be *fused*, or as Paul expressed it later, 'baptised in one Spirit into one body'.[6] Similarly with the 3,000 converts. As they sealed their new-found faith in the dual experience of water baptism and the reception of the Holy Spirit,[7] they not only came into a new relationship with God but also with one another. They discovered community as no people on earth had ever done before. It wasn't that they had planned it that way. God had produced it by the action of the Holy Spirit.

Bricks and timber lying around a building site do not make a building. Brick must be laid upon brick, timber fixed to timber. In other words the art of building involves bringing the various building materials together in a right relationship, according to the design of the architect. To use another scriptural metaphor, a human body will only function properly if its constituent parts are 'joined and knit together'.[8] The structure of the church is a matter of *relationships*. Notice how spontaneously these new relationships were formed and how simply they developed.

We might have expected Luke to tell us that the 3,000 who responded to Peter's word were 'converted' or 'saved' or 'born again'. He simply tells us that they were '*added*'.[9] Added to what? Added as living stones to the newly formed structure, as living members to the functioning body. It was not a question of a few more names added to the church roll, but the effecting of an organic union with the redeemed community that radically affected the life-style of each individual convert.

Luke goes on to describe the outworking of this. 'They devoted themselves to the apostles' teaching and fellowship, to the breaking of bread and the prayers.' None of these activities was individualistic, it was all community. A new milestone had been reached in the history of God's people, and the Holy Spirit celebrated the occasion by striking a new note in the inspired record. Teaching, prayers, even breaking of bread we have had before, but not *fellowship*. Now that the members of the body have been spiritually fused we are introduced for the first time to '*koinonia*'. The word is also rendered in our common version 'communion', 'contribution', 'communication'. The basic meaning is the state of having in common, the shared life, and it applied to material as well as spiritual things.[10]

Examining carefully the record of the early church we search in vain for 'the loner'. Whether it be the leadership or the led, those who travelled or those who were localised, all were related, all were structured, although by no human hand. 'God arranged the organs in the body, each one of them, as He chose.'[11] In describing this new togetherness, note how the Holy Spirit stresses the words 'all' and 'together':

All who believed were *together* and had *all* things in common; and they sold their possessions and goods and distributed them to *all*, as any had need. And day by day, attending the temple *together* and breaking bread in their homes, they partook of food with glad and generous hearts, praising God and having favour with *all* the people.[12]

These believers were an 'all together' company. This is not to suggest that they practised commune living, or had 'extended households'. Such households are not the New Testament norm. To promote them as though they were is to misunderstand community, and to prevent it being effectively and corporately expressed in *the whole* of the local body. Nor did the sharing of their possessions mean that they necessarily relinquished possession of their goods when they joined the Christian community. It says a little later that 'no one said that any of the things which he possessed was his own'.[13] It was not that they did not possess, but that what they possessed was made freely available to others. That is surely the spirit of community.

This openness to one another was one of the open secrets of the power and authority of these first Christians. The tidal wave of blessing that brought in 3,000 on the day of Pentecost now continued in a steady stream of blessing as 'the Lord *added* to their number day by day those who were being saved'. The depth of their commitment to Christ was seen in the depth of their commitment to each other. True spiritual *koinonia* in its manifold forms of expression, is one of the most beautiful fruits of the outpouring of the Spirit.

Henry Groves wrote of the 1860 Revival in South India:

There are now in Christian Pettah alone, about one hundred who are bound together in the ties of Christian fellowship, and in the district of Arulappatoor there is about the same number, and very many more scattered about elsewhere. Sunday they make a day of special fasting and prayer, abstaining often from food till after the partaking of the Lord's Supper, which is partaken of every Sunday evening at eight. They appear to be living in much real simplicity, having all that they have in common, and working together for the common support.[14]

Wherever the Holy Spirit is renewing the church there is talk about community living. This is not surprising as it touches such an important aspect of the life-style of God's kingdom. Most church-goers nowadays meet together once or twice a week, sing a few hymns, 'amen' a few prayers, listen to a sermon, shake hands with a few friends, and return to their insular and independent life till next service. This is far removed from the fellowship of the New Testament churches. Those Christians came to give as well as to get, to participate as well as to appropriate. Deep-seated personal or domestic problems could not be hidden indefinitely behind Bible and hymn book. They exhorted and challenged each other, built each other up, shared each other's food, got involved in each other's personal lives. And this kind of *koinonia* has always tended to reappear in times of revival.

Today it is not only the prophet but the scientist and the philosopher who tell us that 'the writing is on the wall' for our modern civilisation. The structures of our society are crumbling. With all his impressive scientific progress, man has never mastered the basic principles of living. Nothing demonstrates this so forcibly as the breakdown of family life seen in the astronomical figures for divorce and delinquency.

It is so easy here to explain the situation with a well-worn cliché, such as, 'Man cannot be right with man until man has got right with God'. Very true, but it is not likely to impress the man in the street. What will impress him is to see a modern demonstration of what the pagan world of the first century saw in the early church. Such was the *koinonia* of that first church that we find them 'having favour with all the people', and that 'the people held them in high honour'.[15] The world is waiting to see God's alternative society in action. Only a people who have discovered the principles of kingdom living will hold together when God rises to shake mightily the earth.

Already in widely separating branches of the professing church, the spirit of community living is being restored. This will continue and spread. World-wide revival, heralding the return of the King, will be marked by *koinonia*, beginning with the restoration of family relationships. Malachi concludes the Old Testament revelation by informing us that 'before the great and terrible day of the Lord' arrives, will come the prophetic voice of the end-time 'Elijah' to reconcile fathers to children and children to fathers,[16] and thus result in united families. This will finally dispose of the myth of 'the generation gap'. Instead, the family spirit will pervade and characterise the redeemed community.

NOTES

1. Matt. 16:18
2. Matt. 10:34–36
3. Acts 14:4
4. Gal. 3:28
5. Rev. 1:18
6. 1 Cor. 12:13 Eng. RV '*By* one Spirit were we all baptised . . .' (AV, RSV) tends to obscure the meaning. 'In (Gk. en) one Spirit' is the more natural rendering, especially as this is the Greek preposition used in every other reference to 'baptism *in* the Spirit'.
7. Acts 2:38
8. Eph. 4:16
9. Acts 2:41
10. Acts 2:44–45
11. 1 Cor. 12:18
12. Acts 2:44–46
13. Acts 4:32
14. Report in *The Indian Watchman,* July 1860
15. Acts 2:47; 5:13
16. Mal. 4:5–6

14. A NEW STRUCTURE

We have seen in the community living of the first church the beginnings of that new structure that Jesus had said He would build. There was far more in this than simply adopting a community style of living. The relationships established between these disciples, so utterly different from anything they had known in Judaism, was to form a living vessel suitable to receive and use the mighty inflow of the Spirit. Here was an instrument, fitted and equipped by God, to carry out His great kingdom plans.

To us, with knowledge of the subsequent history, the break with the old order was inevitable. But it may not have seemed inevitable to His disciples, although it was implied by several things that Jesus had said. Like most of us they would have had a strong attachment to the religion in which they were reared. True, it had the form without the power. But might not the mighty working of the Spirit that had already brought thousands of them to Christ yet issue in national repentance, and the acclamation of Jesus as the promised Messiah?

The Christians continued to maintain their links with Judaism, worshipping regularly in temple and synagogue.[1] But seizing every opportunity to witness to Jesus,[2] they only stirred up the implacable opposition of the hierarchy, which soon burst into the flames of open and violent persecution. These Jewish believers came to realise that the rebirth and renewal of

Judaism in the way that they had doubtless hoped was a spiritual impossibility. They had come to the parting of the ways.

Early on in our Lord's ministry, as people began to compare His 'good news of the kingdom' message with the doctrine of the scribes and Pharisees, the question was put to Him by the disciples of John, 'Why do we and the Pharisees fast, but your disciples do not fast?' Our Lord answered with a wedding parable in three parts. He wanted them to grasp the fact that the new thing that God was doing was not with a view to repairing the old, but replacing it.[3]

The first part of the parable had to do with the bridegroom and the wedding guests. How could the guests mourn while the bridegroom was with them? Then He spoke of clothing, one of the first things people think about when invited to a wedding. Remember the parable about the man found without a proper wedding garment. In no way could a worn or torn garment be made suitable by patching with a piece of new cloth. Finally, there was the wine – such an important element in a wedding feast, as we learn from that famous one in Cana of Galilee. Wine requires a suitable wineskin.

Jesus was firstly emphasising *joy* as one of the outstanding characteristics of the new order. John the Baptist's ministry was bringing to a close the era known as 'the law and the prophets'. From then on the relevant message would be 'the glad tidings of the kingdom of God'.[4] Gladness was to be the keynote, hence this wedding parable with its emphasis on feasting rather than fasting; on a new, not a patched garment; and on wine that makes glad the heart of man.

How different all this was to the asceticism and austerity that marked the old order of things, and of John's ministry in particular! This was the torn and tattered garment, and it accords with what Hebrews tells us of the old covenant: 'Becoming obselete ... growing old ... ready to vanish away'.[5]

The contrast between the new and the old was vividly portrayed by our Lord when He spoke of children in the market places playing, now weddings, now funerals, and finding no response from their playmates. John had wailed to 'this generation' but they did not mourn. Jesus had piped but they did not dance.[6]

Our Lord used the wedding simile not only because the new era was one of gladness, but because marriage speaks of a new union, a new relationship, a new phase of life begun. This was what our Lord's ministry and the coming of the Spirit were to bring. As Paul expressed it later, Christ's death had broken the old union with the law so that we could now be married to the One who was raised from the dead, and so produce offspring for God.[7]

The pictures of the garment and the wineskin present two aspects of the same truth, and it is a truth we need to hear today. It is that the old and new are fundamentally incompatible. With the garment and the patch the lesson is this: if you try to use the new to patch the old you end up with 'a worse tear'. With the wine and the wineskin the lesson is much the same: put new wine into old wineskins that have lost their flexibility and you destroy the wineskins and lose the wine. Put new wine into new wineskins and both are preserved. With both the garment and the wine the emphasis is on preservation.

The immediate application of the parable is clear. The threadbare garment of Judaism could never be improved by a patching operation, using Christ's kingdom teaching for the purpose. Instead, in the confrontation of Judaism and Christianity that followed, a gaping hole was soon torn in the ancient religion as thousands of devout Jews, including a large number of priests, turned to Christ. The old wineskin could not cope with the potency of the kingdom message, and all that it involved.

Look for a moment at those Jewish Christians after Pentecost. So avid were they for spiritual food that they *devoted themselves* to the apostles' teaching, fellowship, breaking of bread and prayer. There was sobriety and yet exuberant joy. Gifts of the Spirit flowed freely in the meetings. Signs and wonders were accepted as normal. All were at liberty to bring their priestly offerings of worship to God. What praise and liberty filled the homes where they assembled! Though the emergence of synagogue worship, with its eldership and teaching ministry, had begun providentially to replace the ritual of the temple with its priestly hierarchy, and thus prepare the way for the new order, there was no way that it could contain the new thing that God was doing.

Sometimes we find the disciples ejected from the synagogue, and at other times compelled to withdraw.[8] Thus were the first churches born. Soon gifts of leadership, in addition to 'the Twelve' began to emerge. Elders were raised up to rule in the local congregations. The ascended Christ began to give gifts to men, apostles, prophets, evangelists, shepherds and teachers. A simple structure began to appear. The leaders did not form an hierarchy – that had been their major source of trouble in the old structure – but enjoyed a relationship based on love, trust and submission. Out of it they exercised a ministry characterised by spiritual authority. This was the new wineskin of Jesus' parable, wholly suited to the new wine. In this way the outpoured blessing of Pentecost was conserved and enlarged when it could so easily have been dissipated.

Many do not want to see any application of this parable beyond the immediate one of Judaism and Christianity. But its lessons are writ large across the pages of Church history. Our Lord was giving us a pictorial description of every subsequent movement of the Spirit resulting in the recovery of New Testament Christianity. The story of that first century, tragic as far as Judaism was concerned, has been repeated in so many of the later outpourings of the Spirit. Unable to embrace and assimilate the new thing God was doing, the old order gave way, first to jealousy – because heaven was crowning the new with blessing and success; then to fear – because it now felt its own existence threatened by that success; and finally to open hostility.

Most denominational churches, historic or otherwise, had their origin in a distinct movement of the Holy Spirit, involving not only a renewing of life, but a recovery of truth. But Mother Church rejected her offspring, and the new movement was either thrown out or compelled to withdraw, and thus a new expression of the church was born.

The eighteenth-century Awakening in Great Britain under the preaching of Wesley and Whitfield brought a new emphasis on regeneration and holy living. But it was not so much these truths that brought them into conflict with the Establishment. It was the disgusting innovation of preaching the sacred gospel outside a consecrated building! And as for permitting unlettered men, who had never been properly 'ordained' to preach it, who had ever heard of such a thing? What Anglicans and others now accept as normal was viewed by their forebears as a shocking innovation. It is salutary for us to remember that the breaking of these shackles of tradition was won by those early Methodists at the cost of much abuse and persecution. Staid Anglicanism could not then cope with shouting Methodists – it may be easier now as they seem to have stopped shouting! – and the break with the established church that Wesley had foreseen came soon after his death.

Those who are wedded to the old tend inevitably to view the new with dismay. Jesus anticipated this sort of conservatism in the very parable we have been considering. He said, 'No one after drinking old wine desires new; for he says, "The old is good".'[9] If we have been reared in the old it is natural that we long for it to be restored rather than bypassed. The fact is that while revivals have sometimes renewed entire congregations, this has never led to the reviving of the denomination. The making new of the old wineskin is possible congregationally, but not denominationally. But this introduces another factor.

There is no question that God works, often powerfully, in the old structures. But it is inevitable that those very structures put serious limitations on His working. It is all too easy for the ground gained to be lost, for the situation to revert, and for the whole process to need repeating within a short space of time. Take the 1950 Lewis Awakening. Though confined to certain Presbyterian churches in the Outer Hebrides, this was a powerful movement of the Spirit that deeply affected those communities at the time. Many found faith in Christ, and some of these are now in full-time service. But the fact remains that in less than a decade you could visit those very churches where God had worked so powerfully and never suspect that they had ever tasted revival. Without a change of structure it is virtually impossible to conserve the fruits of revival.

But what, it may be asked, is the use of a new structure? Will it not in the process of time harden into another denominational system, develop its own self-interest and protectiveness, and the whole process need to be repeated? We have only to ask ourselves, what would have happened if those first Jewish disciples had been swayed by this kind of argument? Or if it had prevented the reformers from embracing the light that God had given them, even though this resulted in the establishing of new churches? In the early Pentecostal movement at the beginning of this century, many were faced with the grim alternatives of renouncing what they had come to believe and experience, or being ejected from their churches. Were they wrong to choose the latter, even though it did result in the formation of a Pentecostal denomination? We are responsible for what we do with truth revealed to us, but we are not responsible for what future generations do.

In saying all this I am not implying that I agree with the

basic assumption that lies behind this objection, that every
fresh recovery movement of the Holy Spirit is bound to end up
in stagnation. There must come a generation that will complete
the process of recovery and so bring back the King. It could be
this generation. Let us think and act as though it were. If God
presents us with a new way, we must not allow religious nos-
talgia or sentiment to hold us back. Nor must we shrink from
paying the price of obedience to God. To be called 'charismatic'
is almost respectable, but not to be called 'schismatic'. But that
is what they called those first Christians. They were a highly
disreputable break-away movement, and dubbed 'the sect of
the Nazarenes'.[10] In those days just to belong could mean im-
prisonment or death. At this present time the price of obedience
is not so high. But if we should ever be faced with the kind of
alternatives that many have had to face as a result of past
movements of the Spirit, let us make sure we obey God rather
than man, and that we are ruled by the Word, and not by
sentiment or self-interest.

NOTES

1. Luke 24:53; Acts 2:46; 3:1
2. Acts 5:12, 19–21
3. Matt. 9:14–17
4. Luke 16:16
5. Heb. 8:13
6. Matt. 11:16–19
7. Rom. 7:4
8. Acts 19:9
9. Luke 5:39
10. Acts 24:5

15. BREAK UP THAT FALLOW GROUND

The outpouring of the Spirit, as we have already seen, is likened in Scripture to a deluge of rain on a dry and thirsty land. But if that deluge is to result in a harvest, then the soil must first be prepared. 'Break up your fallow ground,' cries the prophet Hosea, 'for it is time to seek the Lord, that He may come and rain righteousness upon you.'[1]

'Break up your fallow ground' is clearly a call for heart preparation. 'It is time to seek the Lord' is a plea for prevailing prayer. And the Lord coming to rain righteousness upon us is heaven's beautiful description of the promised outpouring. This chapter will be devoted to the matter of our own heart preparation, and the one following to the theme of prevailing prayer.

What is fallow ground? It is not desert that has never been cultivated. The application therefore is not to unbelievers who have never experienced God's grace. Nor is it necessarily land that was once cultivated, but has now been abandoned and returned to a desert state. So it is not particularly the backslider who is in view. It is land that has borne fruit in the past, but now lies idle through lack of cultivation. Here is a fitting description of the hearts of many who profess the name of Christ. Like the Corinthians, they are part of 'God's field',[2] but are spiritually unproductive.

Fallow ground is *hard*; that is why it needs to be broken up.

Hardness is not confined to those who have denied the faith or
fallen into deep sin. We can have this state of heart and at the
same time be quite correct in our behaviour and quite orthodox
in our doctrine. In some respects the Pharisees were like that.
The heart that is hard is unresponsive to the word of God. This
is the wayside ground in the parable, trampled by the feet of
men, where the seed fell but never penetrated, and was quickly
devoured by the birds.

Jesus interpreted the wayside as those who heard the word
but did not understand it.[3] Shortly afterwards, following the
feeding of the five thousand, His own disciples illustrated His
point, for we read, 'They did not understand about the loaves,
for their hearts were hardened'.[4] There are believers today sitting under the finest ministry year after year without giving any
evidence of spiritual growth. Their state of heart has deprived
them of spiritual understanding, though their minds are being
filled with biblical information.

The heart that is hard is insensitive to the voice of the Holy
Spirit. There are so many ways in which He speaks, quite apart
from preaching: through people, through illness, through be-
reavement, through financial difficulties, through setbacks,
through accidents, or simply through that 'still small voice'
deep in our conscience. But the insensitive heart does not hear.
There are burdens God wants to share, but He cannot do that if
we are out of touch. There are secrets He would whisper, but
only to hearts that are tender and responsive.

Fallow ground is *weed-bound*. One of the main objects of
cultivation is to eliminate weeds that would overrun the good
seed or the growing plants. 'Break up your fallow ground, and
sow not among thorns,' exhorted Jeremiah.[5] The people did
not heed him, for we learn later that they reaped the thorns that
they had refused to weed out.[6] As every gardener knows, weeds
do not have to be cultivated to thrive. They are the inevitable
product of neglect. If we are not diligently cultivating the

garden of the soul, we may be sure that spiritual 'weeds' are flourishing.

If we would heed the word of the prophet, we must begin humbly and honestly to deal with what we know are 'weeds': the things that grieve the Spirit, check our growth, and hinder the outpouring of the Spirit we so desperately need. It is so easy to excuse our sins by calling them 'short-comings'. It is so easy to attribute them to temperament or environment. We must cease justifying our carnal ways and materialistic outlook by pointing to others who are the same. We must face them openly in the light of God's presence, view them as He does, and deal with them in true repentance.

Finally, fallow ground is *unfruitful*. It may be sown with the finest seed. It may receive copious showers. But the results will be at best disappointing. The supreme reason for which the Lord chose us, and the ultimate purpose of all His dealing with us, is that we may be fruitful. Nothing short of fruit will satisfy Him. His heartbreak over Israel was that when He looked to His vineyard for grapes, large and luscious, grapes to delight His heart, all He found were wild grapes, miserably small and horribly sour.[7]

What were these 'grapes' that God vainly looked for in Israel? Isaiah goes on to tell us, 'He looked for justice . . . for righteousness', for the conduct and character in keeping with those who professed to be the people of God. Does He find it in us? It is possible to be religiously active, even zealous in our service for God, yet when a hungry Saviour comes to us, as to the fig tree, looking for fruit, He finds nothing but the leaves of our busyness. And so He goes His way as hungry as when He came, and deeply disappointed.

What then is to be done with this unproductive fallow ground? We are to break it up, says the prophet. Notice, it is not primarily a question of God breaking us, but of us breaking ourselves. We must be careful not to make the common mistake of putting the onus on God: 'Please break me', when He has already put the onus on us by saying, 'You break your own fallow ground'. Of course we cannot do this without Him. But when He sees us responding to His command in obedience and faith, He will do His part, working in us by His Spirit, and making our response effective.

Breaking up the fallow ground means bringing our hearts to a humble and contrite state before God. This is the state that is ready for the rain of revival. God's ways have not changed since He told His people under the old covenant that He would 'revive the spirit of the humble, and . . . revive the heart of the contrite'.[8] Humbling ourselves is the first step. This gets the blade of the plough into the hard soil. Then comes the contrition that turns the soil over. Have you noticed that God always commands us to humble ourselves?[9] But this is not something that we are able to do without Him. We do it 'under His mighty hand'. It is this that brings the divine pressure to bear upon us. But it is our response that determines whether we are humbled or hardened. This may be seen when God deals with a nation in judgment. Some respond with submission and repentance. Others with stubbornness and rejection. The sun that melts the wax will harden the clay.

It was through temptation to pride that Satan seduced Eve, and so breathed this deadly poison into the human race. Christendom has recognised it as one of 'the seven deadly sins'. There is good ground for calling it 'the deadliest of the deadly', inasmuch as it is so often the root of the others. It is the lifting up and justifying of self before God and man. It is the subtle influence behind many of the works of the flesh. Often it masquerades behind a show of piety, or even of supposed humility. Like the story, no doubt apocryphal, of the man who was so 'humble' that the church gave him a medal, and then had to take it from him because he wore it!

Pride lies behind most disorders and divisions and heresies

in the church. It is the deadly enemy of revival, and one of the most difficult things to diagnose and deal with. We may be guilty of it at the very time our hearts are assuring us that we are free of it. Our safety is to cry out with David, 'Search me, O God.' Our willingness to do so may be the beginning of the process of breaking up our fallow ground.

Humbling ourselves does not mean that we speak disparagingly of ourselves, or deny the gifts or abilities that God has given us. For someone with a gift of administration to say, 'I'm not much good at organising' is to draw forth the response, 'Of course you are', which may well have been the purpose of the exercise! It is usually either an expression of inverted pride, or of deep insecurity. No, humbling ourselves is simply taking our rightful place before God, not thinking of ourselves more highly than we ought to think, but thinking soberly, and acknowledging that we have nothing that we have not received, and that all is of grace.

When we are conscious of guilt or failure, it is pride that causes us to hide away from God among the trees of activity. But when we humble ourselves, we come out from our hiding place, expose our hearts and lives to the searchlight of God's presence, with a willingness to come to grips with reality. We cease trying to justify ourselves at God's expense. Instead, we are ready to take God's side against ourselves.

One of the most significant statements in the whole Bible that sets out the pathway to revival, commences, 'If My people who are called by My name *humble* themselves . . .'[10] We see this in the revival that blessed the reign of Josiah. When he gave the lead to the nation by abasing himself before God, heaven responded at once, 'Because your heart was tender and you humbled yourself before God . . . I also have heard you.'[11] When he broke up his fallow ground God rained on him and the nation the rain of righteousness.

Out of this self-humbling comes *contrition*. The humbling

D

brings us to the place of self-exposure, and then contrition is the acknowledging as true what God then reveals. The Hebrew word translated 'contrite' is deeply significant in the context of breaking up the fallow ground. It means 'bruised' or 'broken to pieces'. Job uses it when defending himself against the accusations of his friends, 'How long will you torment me, and *break me in pieces* with words.'[12] When the words of the Almighty affect us in this way our hearts are truly contrite. Then we have His presence and experience His reviving, as He promised.[8]

Geologists tell us that the soil of the earth is mainly rock, pulverised by the ceaseless action of the elements throughout the millenniums of the past. Even so, the contrite heart is that in which everything rock-like and resistant to the will of God has been pulverised through the power of His word and the working of His providence. It is one of the great benefits of the new covenant that He takes out of us the stony heart and gives us a heart of flesh.[13]

It is so often the unveiling of God to our inner being when we have truly humbled ourselves that brings about this contrition. It was so with Abraham the idolator when the God of glory appeared to him in Ur of the Chaldees. It was so with Moses when God appeared to him in a flame out of the midst of a bush. It was so with Joshua when, approaching Jericho, he met the Captain of the Lord's Host. It was so with Isaiah when he saw the Lord sitting on His throne, high and lifted up. And it was so with Job when God spoke to him out of the whirlwind. It puts us on our faces, and wrings from our lips the cry, 'Woe is me', 'I abhor myself and repent', or 'What does my Lord bid His servant?'

Contrition, as we have seen, is a state of repentance, and all true repentance involves confession, without which there can be no forgiveness or cleansing. Confession is an act of identification. When we confess Christ we identify ourselves with Him. When we confess sin we identify ourselves with the sin. We point to it and say, 'Lord, that's me.' Since all sin is primarily against Him, there must always be confession to Him. But where others have been affected or wronged, then we must confess to them also. Jesus taught us that God cannot accept our gift, our offering of worship or of service, if we know that our brother has something against us. I must leave my gift at the altar, as a token to God of my sincerity, seek out my brother and put things right, and then come and offer my gift.[14]

There is a time and place for public confession of sin, and it is a characteristic of the powerful working of the Spirit in times of revival. God often uses it to spread conviction, whether among believers or unbelievers, and to deepen the work. But leaders need to watch for spurious confession, which is sensational and attention-seeking, and the detailed confession of moral impurity which defiles the minds of the listeners.[15] The sensitivity of the Holy Spirit is needed when confessing to another whom we have wronged, that we do not wound by our confession. To say to my brother, 'I'm so sorry that I told Brother Smith you were a "big head",' is a back-hander. All I need say is, 'The Holy Spirit has convicted me of speaking disparagingly of you. I am so sorry and ask your forgiveness.'

Sometimes confession must be accompanied by restitution, that is, the restoring of that which we have wrongly obtained or retained. It involves undoing, as far as possible, the result of every wrong that has affected others. Money misappropriated must be returned with interest. If it involves goods, we may have to make financial restitution, to an equivalent value, plus interest. Everything not put right now will be put right at the judgment seat of Christ, when 'the wrongdoer will be paid back for the wrong that he has done'.[16]

There is no state of soil more satisfying to the gardener than that which crumbles at a touch. Even so there is no state of heart more satisfying to God than that which breaks at His touch and crumbles under His strong yet tender hand. 'The sacrifice *acceptable* to God is a broken spirit' – and He will not be bought off with any substitute – 'a broken and contrite heart, O God, *thou* wilt not despise',[17] even if others do.

Just as breaking up the fallow ground is not the coming of the showers, so spiritual brokenness is not revival, but an indispensable step towards it. Hosea reminds us that heart preparation is vital because 'it is time to seek the Lord'. Without this state of heart we cannot seek the Lord aright, we cannot pray in the Spirit. Scripture and history confirm that when the fallow ground is thoroughly broken, and out of that brokenness cries out to heaven, the showers will not be long delayed.

NOTES

1. Hos. 10:12
2. 1 Cor. 3:9
3. Matt. 13:19
4. Mark 6:52
5. Jer. 4:3
6. Jer. 12:13
7. Isa. 5:1–7
8. Isa. 57:15
9. 1 Pet. 5:6; Jas. 4:10
10. 2 Chron. 7:14
11. 2 Chron. 34:27
12. Job 19:2
13. Ezek. 36:26
14. Matt. 5:23–24
15. Eph. 5:12
16. Col. 3:25
17. Ps. 51:17

16. PRAY THROUGH

He was an exile, far away from his native land, yet holding a responsible position in the Persian court. When he heard of the sorry state of his fellow countrymen in the homeland, he reacted deeply. We see in Nehemiah a vivid demonstration of Hosea's word about breaking up one's fallow ground and seeking God for a downpour of righteousness. The one cannot be separated from the other. The kind of praying we are talking about will only flow from prepared hearts. There is an air of self-sufficiency about a field lying fallow. It holds its moisture and feels no need of rain. But once broken up it becomes thirsty and cries to heaven for showers. We see this in Nehemiah.

'The survivors . . . who escaped exile,' they told him, 'are in great trouble and shame; the wall of Jerusalem is broken down, and its gates are destroyed by fire'.[1] See the reaction of the man who had broken up his fallow ground: 'When I heard these words I sat down and wept, and mourned for days; and I continued fasting and praying before the God of heaven.' We do not read of any of the other Jewish exiles reacting in this way. Nehemiah himself could so easily have quietened his conscience and soothed his feelings with the thought that Jerusalem was far away, that he was well cared for in the Persian palace, and that, in any case, the situation in Jerusalem was no fault of his. It was *the people's* sin – the *other* people. But here we see a heart that was sensitive and submissive to God, and in which the Holy Spirit was able to move deeply. These were the labour pains out of which a new movement of God was to be born.

It was as though Nehemiah was seeing this need, not through the eyes of the men who reported it, but through the eyes of God. He felt the burning reproach of a people, once strong and free, and enjoying God's blessing, but now weak, bowed down and utterly despised. But it was not because they were *his* people, but because they were *God's*, and called by *His* name. Their reproach was *God's* reproach. His glory was involved. Every revival movement is a reaction by God to safeguard His own glory. 'It is not for your sake . . . that I am about to act,' God informed Israel, 'but for the sake of my holy name.'[2]

Nehemiah wept and mourned. Revivals have always flowed out of praying, but not of the cold, formal and tearless variety. His heart had been ploughed deep, and was now ready to share the heart of God. Probably he had never before experienced the convulsive sobbing that came upon him, and was at a loss to understand why he felt the way he did. It was simply the Holy Spirit reproducing in him the heartbreak of God over the state of His people.

Tears that spring from the activity of the Holy Spirit are not to be written off as the expression of someone who is a little over-emotional. They have spiritual value and significance, but they must lead on to something more. 'I fasted and prayed before the God of heaven,' recorded Nehemiah. I do not know of any significant movement of the Spirit in any part of the world that was not precipitated by prayer. Whether it was a lone intercessor with a burden from God, or a handful who stood as watchmen on the walls, or a widespread movement of prayer, as with the great American Revival of 1858, prayer has always prepared the way of the Lord.

With the strong emphasis that the Spirit of God is now bringing to the church, that God's people are a functioning

community, that He does not want us to act in independence
but only in relationship, it is not surprising that we do not hear
much nowadays of movements of the Spirit being born out of
some individual's personal burden and special ministry of
intercession. The emphasis is clearly on community praying,
where two or more agree together in the Spirit concerning that
which they ask, and claim the answer that Jesus promised, 'It
shall be done.' But it must be emphasised that this spirit of
prayer cannot be worked up at will. It comes from the Spirit of
God to the prepared heart.

When it says that Nehemiah fasted as well as prayed, it
means that he went without his food. It is necessary to make
this point, as the modern tendency is to spiritualise a biblical
practice like fasting, because we don't like the thought of taking
it too literally. It isn't according to our tradition, and anyway,
wasn't it taken to excess in the medieval church? So we say,
'Fasting is to abstain from anything that hinders our communion with God,' or 'Fasting means to do without, to practise
self-denial.' You have only to widen the meaning enough and
the cutting edge has gone. The result is that we fall into a
position that is as extreme as the ascetic fasting of medievalism.
It is the extreme of never doing any real fasting at all!

Not only do we find many great Old Testament saints
fasting in times of great pressure and need, but it was also
practised by Christ and His apostles. In church history we find
great reformers, scholars, ministers and missionaries are numbered amongst those who fasted as well as prayed, and testified
to the value of the practice. But we come back to the teaching of
our Lord Himself, who said in His great treatise on the principles of the kingdom, '*When* you fast,' this is how you are to do
it. He did *not* say, '*If* you fast.' He assumed that there would be
times when we would feel our need to seek God in this way.

What then is the purpose of fasting? For a full treatment on
what the Bible has to teach us about the subject, the reader

might refer to my book, *God's Chosen Fast.*[3] In a word, it is a divinely appointed means of sharpening our intercession. It makes our prayers more focused and so more forceful. It gives heaven notice that we mean business, that we do not intend to take 'No' for an answer. It is not surprising, therefore, that prayer and fasting have preceded many a revival.

Hosea exhorts us 'to seek the Lord *until* He comes to rain righteousness on you'. It is that little word 'until' that emphasises the need to prevail in prayer, to pray through. This may mean coming into full assurance of faith in prayer so that before the answer is seen you know you have been heard and have already received by faith the thing for which you pray. This is what our Lord meant when He said, 'Whatever you ask in prayer, believe that you *have received* it (Greek past tense), and you will.'[4] Here is a spiritual paradox. You receive it without having actually got it!

When I first received the blessing of the Spirit I searched the Scriptures for three weeks to know whether these things that I had heard about the Holy Spirit were so. God did not permit me to confer with flesh and blood, or to read what other men had to say about the matter. He convinced me from His word alone. Then I earnestly prayed that His Spirit would come upon me. I knew nothing about the laying on of hands, and in any case at that time there was no one I knew to whom I could turn for such ministry. But one evening God gave me through His word an absolute assurance that He had heard my prayer. I said to my wife, 'I've got it!' She replied, 'What have you got?' That was difficult, for I had nothing to show, or to which I could testify, simply the assurance that my praying had been met by an 'Amen' in heaven.

I was like an employee who, as he collected his pay, asked the boss about the possibility of a rise. To his delight the boss agreed. On reaching home he announces to his wife, 'I've got my rise.' 'That's great,' she replies, 'I've already over-spent my housekeeping this week.' 'Wait a moment, dear, I haven't got it yet. I only spoke to the boss today.' The man had it, and yet he didn't have it. What he had was the boss's word. That's where I was. I had received heaven's invoice informing me that my order had been despatched. Now I had only to wait expectantly for the delivery of the goods. What I could *not* do was to put in another order. I was sure God had the matter in hand, and so I never asked Him again. Thanksgiving took over from supplication, and in less than a couple of days I was filled. Often in praying for revival there is a point where we receive in faith, followed by a waiting time, and then we receive in reality.

However, this is not the only way of praying through. Sometimes it pleases God to surprise us with His answer. As with the church in Jerusalem praying for Peter's release from prison, they were still engaged in earnest, persistent prayer when Peter himself knocked on the door. I do not think for a moment they were in unbelief, but not having any prior assurance that they had prayed through, they could not believe the answer had come. So it is sometimes in revival; the saints at prayer are surprised when the blessed event overtakes them. They had prayed through before they knew it. Praying through, then, is to pray until we either see the answer, or have the full assurance that it is on the way.

Returning to Nehemiah, his recorded prayer is surely one of the most outstanding in Scripture. Great was his concept of the need, but greater by far his concept of the God who would meet it. 'O Lord God of heaven, the great and terrible God who keeps covenant and steadfast love with those who love Him and keep His commandments.' He is filled with holy fear at the sense of the majesty, greatness and power of God. But this God is not aloof and unapproachable, for He 'keeps covenant and steadfast love' with those who love and obey Him. He is a God who may be approached with confidence, for He is true to His promises.

Reminding God of His covenant engagements is a vital element in effective intercession. Abraham, Moses, Elijah, Daniel, and many others used this spiritual lever. It would be true to say that all the intercession that down the ages has shaken the kingdom of darkness has been based on the promises of God. Why should we expect Him to do something He has not promised to do? How dare we make Him a liar by not believing He will do what He has promised? It is the promise of the Spirit's outpouring, quickened to us by God, that becomes the fuel of revival praying.

The major obstacle in God answering Nehemiah's prayer for the reviving and restoring of His people was the people's sin. This was not something to be glossed over but laid open before God in confession. This Nehemiah did. 'Confessing the sins of the people of Israel, which we have sinned against Thee.' Confession of sin is a characteristic feature of revival praying. This servant of God could not force others to confess, but he could confess for them and identify himself with their sin, by acknowledging that he and his father's house had added their own quota to the iniquities that had turned God's face from them. God had said, 'If you return to Me . . . I will gather you.' Here then is one man returning, but many more will follow.

Finally, the praying of Nehemiah had produced in him a readiness for all that the answer to his prayer involved. We hinder the answer if we are not willing for such involvement. Praying through includes praying *ourselves* through to the place where we are ready to do whatever God may require of us. For Nehemiah it was to mean a difficult and dangerous path. Time and again he would have to take his life in his hands. Back in Jerusalem the enemy was waiting to stir up a hornet's nest. Even amongst those committed to this work of restoration there would be dissension and difficulty. But God had worked in this man a steadfast determination to go through with the task.

During those forty years in the land of Midian, Moses had no doubt offered a thousand prayers for the deliverance of His people languishing in Egyptian slavery. How his heart must have leapt when God said to him at the burning bush, 'I have come down to deliver them.' Here at last was the answer. But what a bombshell when He added, 'Come, I will send *you* to Pharaoh that *you* may bring forth My people.' 'Oh, no Lord, not that!' The disciples had the same lesson to learn when the Lord commanded them to pray for the sending of labourers into the harvest, for in the next verse He sent them out to be the answer to their own prayers. We need to beware of revival praying! It may well end up with the cry, 'Lord, what wilt Thou have me to do?' But if we mean business we shall be determined to pray through and go through.

NOTES

1. Neh. 1:3
2. Ezek. 36:22
3. *God's Chosen Fast—A Spiritual and Practical Guide to Fasting* by Arthur Wallis, a paperback published by Kingsway
4. Mark 11:24

17. THE SOUND OF MARCHING

Soon after David had been acknowledged as king over all Israel he was threatened by the Philistines.[1] They occupied the valley of Rephaim. After first asking God if he should go against them David led a bold frontal attack that carried the day. Later the Philistines returned and took up the same position. Without presuming on earlier guidance or past success David again asked God. This time he was told to make a detour and take up a position behind them, near the balsam trees. God said, 'When you hear the sound of marching in the tops of the balsam trees, then bestir yourself; for the Lord has gone out before you to smite the army of the Philistines.'

These two battles illustrate a significant difference between the normal operations of the Spirit of God through the church, and His operation in revival. In the first we see man acting under God's direction and with His enabling. In the second it is God who takes the field and smites the Philistines, and man has little to do but gather the spoils of victory. But for the moment we are simply concerned to notice that God gave David a sign, 'the sound of marching in the tops of the balsam trees', to acquaint him with the fact that He Himself had intervened and that the heavenly armies were being thrown into the conflict.

Just as there are signs given us by our Lord to warn us of the imminence of His return, so Scripture also gives us signs encouraging us to believe that the Lord is about to intervene by

His mighty Spirit. We need to be careful here that we do not look in the wrong direction. In the early days of the Salvation Army in France, the eldest daughter of General Booth, who was always afterwards known by her French rank, the 'Maréchale', was put in charge of the work in Paris. She found it very hard and wrote to tell the old General of her discouragement. His advice was, 'Take your eyes off the waves and fix them on the tide.' To be preoccupied with the waves, with the local advances and retreats, is to be alternately elated and dejected. This completely undermines faith. Is the tide rising? That is the question that matters. What are the signs that should alert us that God is about to visit us? Do we see them today?

The first is *a spirit of lawlessness and deadness*. It is a big mistake if we are expecting to see revival heralded by a decrease of evil in society and a general improvement in the state of the church. The very reverse is often the case. 'It is time for the Lord to act,' cried the Psalmist, 'for Thy law has been broken.'[2] Jonathan Edwards wrote from his experience of the New England Revival, 'How dead a time it was everywhere before this work began.'[3] Shortly after the 1904 Revival broke out, a correspondent of the *Liverpool Daily Post* wrote in that paper: 'If I had been asked a month ago whether a revival was probable in Wales, I should have answered, "No". It seemed to me that the "higher criticism" had wrecked the ordinary machinery of a revival.'[4]

So prevailing deadness among believers and abounding lawlessness in the world are not an indication that revival is impossible but that it is imperative. To the Psalmist the very hopelessness of the situation was one of the strongest arguments in favour of divine intervention. He saw in the very situation a challenge that an omnipotent God could not ignore. The very need of the hour cried out, 'It is time for the Lord to work.'

Then there is *a spirit of dissatisfaction*. This may be wide-spread or confined to a few of God's people, but it is something that spreads and grows. Here are the first birth pangs out of which revival is born. The period preceding a spiritual awakening

> is characterised by a profound sense of dissatisfaction awaking in many hearts. A period of gloom sets in, a weariness and exhaustion invade the heart, the pleasures of the world no longer satisfy . . . Slowly this aching grows, the heart of man begins to cry out for God, for spiritual certainties, for fresh visions. From a faint desire this multiplies as it widens, until it becomes a vast human need; until in its urgency it seems to beat with violence at the very gates of heaven.[5]

In the time preceding revival, when coldness, apathy and complacency seem to abound, the Holy Spirit comes to 'disturb this sleep of death'. He produces at first a spiritual restlessness, though it may be only in the hearts of a few. They cannot be satisfied with a holding operation, with the maintaining of the status quo. They sense in their hearts that God must have some better thing for His people. This dissatisfaction becomes a thirst. Did not God say, 'I will pour water upon Him that is thirsty, and streams upon the dry ground?'[6] Did not Jesus pronounce blessedness on those who hungered and thirsted for righteousness, and promise that they shall be filled? The outpouring of the Spirit is born out of soul-thirst.

There is a thirst for God to manifest Himself, for His power and glory to be displayed. Believers begin to view with growing concern their own spiritual ineffectiveness. They are aware, as was David, of the taunting of the world, 'Where is this God of yours?' They respond also with David's heart-cry, 'My soul thirsteth for Thee . . . to see Thy power and Thy glory'.[7] Or they plead, as did the prophet, 'O that Thou wouldst rend the heavens and come down.'[8] The more they examine the pages of the New Testament and the lives of those whom God has used, the more convinced they become that they themselves, and the church of which they form a part, are living a Christianity that is sub-standard.

This dissatisfaction is further fed as they read of the mighty things that happened in days gone by through the outpouring of the Spirit. They hear of what God is doing today in other parts of the world. 'If He is still in the business, why is He not working like that here? And where are all the signs and the wonders, the healings and the miracles that the early Christians accepted as normal, and that have so often recurred in times of revival?' There is a sensing that the 'no miracles today' theory is a clumsy attempt to cover up our own unbelief and spiritual deficiency.

Closely associated with this sense of dissatisfaction, and often springing directly out of it is *a new sensitivity to sin.* You will notice that most of these signs of impending blessing are simply anticipating in the hearts of the few, what will become a general characteristic when the outpouring of the Spirit eventually comes. The God who dwells in 'the high and holy place' has promised to 'revive the spirit of the humble, and to revive the heart of the contrite'.[9] So the mark of a humble and contrite spirit among God's people is an indication that they are being prepared for a significant work of the Holy Spirit.

This deep conviction of sin is usually evidenced by public confession. Christians are not easily brought to the point where they are prepared to obey the injunction, 'Confess your sins to one another, and pray for one another,'[10] to apologise and ask for forgiveness, and to make restitution. Where this happens you may be sure that there is a powerful work of the Holy Spirit going on. But repentance, brokenness, confession, and even making restitution, is not itself revival. It is only the path to it. God revives the contrite. To humble ourselves and confess is what *we* have to do, but to revive is the sole prerogative of God.

Then there is *a spirit of deep concern.* There never seems to be any lack amongst God's people of able and vocal critics of the spiritual state of the church and the moral state of the world. But when that harsh unfeeling criticism gives place to a deep concern that expresses something of the heartache of God, such as we saw in Nehemiah, then we may be sure that God's hour to work has come. This is beautifully expressed by the Psalmist: 'Thou wilt arise and have pity on Zion; it is the time to favour her; the appointed time has come. For Thy servants hold her stones dear, and have pity on her dust.'[11] When God finds those who are as concerned about the stones and dust of Zion, as were Ezra, Nehemiah and Dannel, it will not be long before those that mourn are comforted – by divine intervention.

There is also *a spirit of expectancy.* This brings in the vital faith element, always in evidence in times preceding revival. The stimulus to this faith is provided by those whom we may call 'the watchmen on the walls'. Watchmen are the ones who see the first grey streaks of dawn. It was only 'a little cloud like a man's hand', but to Elijah, 'the watchman' on the top of Carmel, it was the earnest of the heavens 'black with clouds and wind'. When all Ahab could hear was the sighing of the wind in the trees as he sheltered from the blistering heat, Elijah could boldly declare, 'There is a sound of the rushing of rain. King Ahab, you had better prepare your chariot and head for home, or you'll get drenched.'

It is to the eye of the seer or the ear of the intercessor that the first intimation of rain from heaven usually comes. 'Behold, the former things have come to pass, and new things I now declare; before they spring forth I tell you of them.'[12] Charles Finney recounts the story of a woman in New Jersey who was positive there was going to be a revival. She wanted special meetings arranged, but the minister and elders were unresponsive. They

saw nothing to encourage this expectation. So she went ahead
and got a carpenter to make seats so she could have meetings in
her house. She had scarcely opened her doors before the Spirit
of God came down with great power, and these sleepy members
found themselves in the midst of convicted sinners. They could
only exclaim, 'Surely the Lord was in this place, and we knew it
not.' How could this woman be so sure? Simply because she
was one of those watching and waiting, and she had heard from
God.

Another mark is *a spirit of unity* amongst believers. 'With
one accord' characterised the preparation of those early disciples for the first outpouring of the Holy Spirit, and generally
speaking, this is how it has been with every subsequent outpouring. We are all aware that strife and contention, bitterness
and jealousy within the Christian community is one of the
devil's most effective means of hindering the work of the Holy
Spirit. Seldom is there a local break-through until such a situation is remedied. So it is in the wider setting. So long as there
is fear and mistrust between churches, jealousy and com-
petition, and the ostracising of one another, it is not likely that
God will visit that circle of churches with revival.

I am not saying that God always waits until all the communities of His people are one before He will pour out His
Spirit. If that were so I question if there would ever have been
a history of revivals. Sometimes a separation amongst God's
people is indispensable to the fulfilling of God's purpose.
Though Scripture describes Lot as 'that righteous man', God
had to break Abraham's working relationship with him before
he could reveal to the patriarch His full purpose. But observe,
there was no acrimony in their parting. With the division of the
kingdom in the reign of Reheboam, though there were in-
justices at the root of the matter, God did not permit Reheboam to take any steps to restore the Northern Kingdom to
his rule. He simply said, 'This thing is from Me.' The break-up

of the working relationship between Paul and Barnabas, though
it came out of a 'sharp disagreement' over John Mark, resulted
in the forming of another apostolic team. Later we find Paul
acknowledging that this young man, with whom earlier he had
not been prepared to work, was useful to him for ministry.

We are being much too simplistic if we conclude that all
division among God's people must be wrong. That depends on
a lot of factors. It has relevance to the question of whether God
requires us to remain in the churches in which we happened to
be reared. We cannot answer this by rule of thumb. In Ezekiel's
vision of the valley of dry bones, there was a shaking and bone
came to his bone. If I am not joined in God to the right bone
there may have to be a shaking and a breaking that God may be
able to set me where He wants me to be. We must all agree that
this is God's prerogative because He 'arranged the organs in the
body, each one of them, as He chose'.[13]

The fact remains that carnal division is a major blockage to
the Spirit's moving, and when we see all this beginning to
break down, replaced by a spirit of unity and love, then we may
take heart in the knowledge that we are witnessing a characteristic sign of impending revival. 'Behold, how good and
pleasant it is when brothers dwell in unity! ... For there the
Lord has commanded the blessing.'[14]

Then *a conviction of coming persecution* is presumptive evidence that God will visit His people in revival. The story of
Pentecost and its aftermath, and the history of many subsequent revivals teach us that God's usual way of preparing His
people for persecution is to pour out His Holy Spirit on them.
In recent years revivals have preceded seasons of great trial in
Belgian Congo (now Zaire), in Korea, in Ethiopia and in many
other places. For the past few years a prophetic voice has been
sounding through many lips in the countries of the West, warning us that persecution is coming. We have had it so easy for so
long that we have almost forgotten that this is normal. New

Testament experience. We shall not be discouraged if we remember that the outpouring of the Spirit that precedes it, that may even precipitate it, is also normal New Testament experience, and part of God's programme.

Finally, there is *the spirit of intercession*, dealt with in an earlier chapter. I think we may confidently say that revival never comes without this 'forerunner' preparing the way. As Matthew Henry, the Puritan commentator, quaintly put it, 'When God intends great mercy for His people, the first thing He does is to set them a praying.' It was Dr. A. T. Pierson's conviction, that 'From the day of Pentecost, there has been not one great spiritual awakening in any land which has not begun in a union of prayer, though only among two or three; no such outward, upward movement has continued after such prayer meetings have declined.' In other words, revivals are born out of prayer and sustained by prayer. The opening chapters of the Acts certainly illustrate this.

To the religionists of His day our Lord had to say, 'You know how to interpret the appearance of the sky, but you cannot interpret the signs of the times.'[15] Those words were spoken probably only a few months before that first great outpouring of the Spirit. They were quick to see in the darkening cloud the coming of rain, but were blind to all those things around them that heralded the mighty showers of the Spirit. May God open our eyes to see the little cloud arising. Or open our ears to hear the sound of marching. May we respond by seeking Him till He pours down the rain of righteousness. Then the break-through of the Spirit will not find us unprepared, but a people willing in the day of God's power.

Notes

1. 2 Sam. 5:17–25
2. Ps. 119:126
3. *Thoughts on the Revival of Religion in New England* (1742) by Jonathan Edwards
4. Quoted in *Rent Heavens* by R. B. Jones
5. Quoted from *Revivals their Laws and Leaders* by James Burns
6. Isa. 44:3 RV
7. Ps. 63:1–2 RV
8. Isa. 64:1
9. Isa. 57:15
10. Jas. 5:16
11. Ps. 102:13–14
12. Isa. 42:9
13. 1 Cor. 12:18
14. Ps. 133
15. Matt. 16:3

18. THE REVIVAL OF TOMORROW

God has a programme. He does not act haphazardly. He never has to take emergency action. He works according to that which He has planned from before the foundation of the world. And He has never left His people in the dark concerning His intentions. Amos reminds us of this: 'Surely the Lord God does nothing, without revealing His secret to His servants the prophets.'[1] Then, as Habakkuk tells us, the prophet has to 'Write the vision; and make it plain . . . so he may run who reads it'.[2] If we do not have the vision it is impossible to 'run' with certainty. It is the special ministry of the Holy Spirit to help us to understand God's future programme: 'He will guide you into all truth . . . and He will declare to you the things that are to come.'[3]

Success is also one of God's attributes. He 'accomplishes all things according to the counsel of His will'.[4] Everything He plans He carries through to success. 'Has He said, and will He not do it? Or has He spoken, and will He not fulfil it?'[5] Only God can declare with boundless confidence, 'My word . . . shall accomplish that which I purpose, and prosper in the thing for which I sent it.'[6] Joshua reminded Israel, 'Not one thing has failed of all the good things which the Lord your God promised concerning you; all have come to pass for you.'[7]

All who are involved in the work of the kingdom must know that they are committed to a work that is destined to succeed, simply because it is God's. The Almighty has no intention of presiding over the disintegration of His kingdom. How could His armies, earthly or heavenly, be routed when He, the Lord of Armies (Hosts), is at their head? The immediate situation may be as dark as night to the human eye, but to the eye of faith all is bright. We have taken a peep at the end of the Book and know for sure that our Captain wins the last battle!

One of the great truths that the Holy Spirit is now emphasising is that Jesus reigns. Not simply in some golden age of the future, but *now*. This is a key to help us unlock God's future programme. When the Father invited Him to sit at His right hand, it was not because He needed a rest after His great earthly mission. It was an invitation to reign. Not as a mere figure-head. Not as a sovereign who carries the title but has been divested of all executive authority. On the contrary, He reigns as one who has received all authority in heaven and on earth. He reigns in the midst of His foes until those foes have been made His footstool.[8] By and large the professing church has failed to grasp this truth. We have assumed that He must first return to make His enemies His footstool, and then reign. But this word of the Father requires Him to sit and reign until His enemies are made His footstool, and then return.

This is not an Old Testament view that we have to modify in the light of the fuller New Testament revelation. Paul leaves us in no doubt that Christ subdues His enemies, not by His returning but by His reigning: 'For He must reign until He has put all His enemies under His feet.'[9] The writer to the Hebrews is even more explicit when he tells us that Christ 'sat down at the right hand of God, then to wait until His enemies should be made a stool for His feet'.[10]

The church is Christ's ruling instrument on earth. He rules by His Spirit through the people who are now seated with Him in the heavenly places. So His coming again is not that He may succeed where the church has failed, but that He may celebrate the victory the church has won! – although only by His grace and through the mighty operation of His Spirit.

This truth of Christ's present reign is solid ground for spiritual optimism. Paul certainly thought so, for writing a word of encouragement to New Testament believers, he quotes Isaiah: 'The root of Jesse . . . will arise to rule over the nations; the Gentiles will *hope* in Him.' But when will this take place, and who are these Gentiles who will hope in the reigning Christ? The time is now, and the Gentiles included the very Romans to whom Paul was writing, for he applies his quotation to them by saying, 'May *the God of hope* fill *you* with all joy and peace in believing, so that by the power of the Holy Spirit you may *abound in hope.*'[11] And whenever God's people grasp the nature of Christ's present reign, and see in faith its victorious outcome, they find it easy to hope.

That sudden effusion of the Spirit that we call revival is one of the most powerful weapons God uses to further His kingdom plans. We should never view the outpouring of the Spirit as an end in itself, but always in the context of the on-going work of God's kingdom. It should not therefore be any surprise to find that the Bible not only encourages us to be hopeful about the ultimate success of the kingdom, but also about the prospects of coming revival.

On the occasion of that first great outpouring we noted how Peter was inspired by the Holy Spirit to link that event to the Joel prophecy. He applied it to 'the last days', that is, the age of the church, which had its commencement at Pentecost. But the prophecy quoted by Peter stretched right on to the last of 'the last days', that is, to the end of the church age, to the period immediately prior to 'the day of the Lord'. God said:

I will show wonders in the heaven above and signs on the earth beneath, blood, and fire, and vapour of smoke; the sun shall be turned into darkness and the moon into blood, *before*

the day of the Lord comes, the great and manifest day. And
it shall be that whoever calls on the name of the Lord shall be
saved.[12]

Since the signs and wonders mentioned by Peter do not
appear to have been fulfilled either at Pentecost or in subsequent outpourings, we may assume that the final and complete fulfilment of this prophecy is still future, to take place
sometime before the day of the Lord, that is, the Lord's descent
from heaven. As well as the visions, dreams and prophesyings,
the signs and the wonders, it is to be a time characterised by
people finding immediate salvation by calling on the name of
the Lord. This harmonises with what we know of the outpourings of the past. They have been times of great reaping. It
harmonises too with the fact that our Lord associated 'the end
of the age' with the time of harvest.

It is important that we do not stop at the 'harvest' aspect of
revival, inspiring as that is, but look beyond to God's ultimate
purpose. This involves more than saving souls from hell, indispensable as that is. More even than bringing individuals into a
'renewal' experience of the filling, the gifts, or even the sanc-
tifying of the Spirit. It involves a work amongst God's people
that is corporate. 'The body of Christ' has to come to full
maturity, and so become 'the bride' prepared for her husband.
This necessitates the breaking down of every structure that
hinders the unity of Christ's body. If there is one truth that
Paul emphasises and re-emphasises in his teaching on the
church, it is that the body of Christ is one. 'There is one body',
not a multiplicity; just as certainly as 'there is one Spirit', not a
diversity of spirits animating that body; and all this is crucial
to 'the one hope that belongs to your call'.[13] The hope cannot be
fulfilled until the great prayer of Jesus is answered by the unity
of the Godhead being reflected in the unity of the church, and

in such a way that it will be seen and recognised by the world.[14]

At the dawn of the Christian era a Man walked this earth who delighted the heart of God. Through His human and physical body He displayed the power and glory of God. Here at last was 'man' as God intended him to be. The world rejected this manifestation of God in human form. They did away with Him. But God raised Him up, exalted Him to the throne of the universe, and sent down on the waiting band of His disciples the promised Holy Spirit. Christ's physical body on earth had been replaced by a spiritual body, the church, to continue what He had begun.

Before this age closes the world is again to see 'a man' striding the earth, having come to the fulness of his manhood. Not the individual Christ but the corporate Christ. The spiritual body in union with the unseen Head, but having come to 'a mature man, to the measure of the stature which belongs to the fulness of Christ',[15] and displaying throughout the earth the power and glory of God, just as Jesus did at the beginning. This is God's supreme purpose for this age. The process began at Pentecost. It will reach its glorious climax in the final outpourings of the age.

Revivals are surely the most powerful single means by which God matures the church. There is limitless potential in every outpouring. Sadly, and for various human reasons, movements are often arrested before their full purpose has been achieved. Some revivals seem to be solely renewal movements. Sinners are converted, sometimes in vast numbers, believers are quickened, and churches renewed. For such wonderful visitations one must profoundly thank God, but they tend to affect the church like a shot in the arm.

If leaders are only looking for the reviving of their own churches, or the prosperity of their own denominations; if there

is no heart longing for the true unity and maturing of the body;
if, despite expressions and demonstrations of unity at the time
of revival, the axe is never laid to the root of sectarianism, the
churches will soon revert to type, return to their denominational enclaves, and within a generation the whole process
will need to be repeated. This was all too apparent in the aftermath of the great 1904 Awakening in Wales. Within one generation the effects of revival in the main-line churches had largely
disappeared.

I said at the beginning of the book that I had learned much
by prayers for revival, often fervent and prolonged, that God
has *not* answered. In the mid-fifties there was in many parts of
the British Isles a stirring to pray for a movement of the Spirit,
stimulated by news of the awakening in the Isle of Lewis, off
the west coast of Scotland. I believe many were expecting God
to work in a similar way in their own situations. God did not
answer those prayers. He seemed reluctant to fulfil the expectations they expressed. Had He done so I believe we would
have had a renewal type revival with short-term results. Despite the mistaken expectations, I believe God was paying those
prayers into another account, that will prove to be much more
significant for the final goal.

Over those same years there sprang up revival fellowships in
a number of the historic denominations, each dedicated to pray
for revival in its own denomination. Not only have these
prayers not been answered, but these fellowships have never
really grown and prospered, and at least two of them have
disbanded. God was seemingly making plain that this was not
the direction in which the wind of His Spirit was blowing.

What then are we to look for in the revival of tomorrow? Of
course we want to see the people of God set on fire. We want to
know that overwhelming sense of God's presence which brings
the fear of the Lord. We are expecting too that powerful impact
on the secular community, resulting in multitudes converted,

baptised and filled with the Holy Spirit. We are looking for signs and wonders, miracles and healings performed in the name of Jesus. But we are also expecting that many will begin to share God's heart in relation to His church. That there will be a willingness for reformation and recovery, for man-made structures and ecclesiastical appointments to be replaced by relationships resulting from bone coming to bone in the body, and the recognition of the anointing of the Spirit as the only qualification for ministry.

I believe that in the coming revival God will not only anoint and thrust forth evangelists, shepherds and teachers, but also apostles and prophets, who are needed as much as they ever were for the perfecting of the saints to their work of ministry, and the general building up of Christ's body. It will be a time of sorting out for many of God's servants who are frustrated in their ministry because they have not found their true rôle. It will get square pegs out of round holes, and put them where they belong. Many in full-time service will find God directing them to return to secular employment, and many in secular employment will be thrust out into full-time service. It will be a time of shaking as the Spirit of God brings adjustment to dislocated members of the body.

At present there is inevitable tension between leaders in denominational churches and those who are leaders in the new undenominational churches that are rising up in the wake of the movement of the Spirit. The old always tends to be fearful and suspicious of the new, and to feel threatened if it grows and prospers. On the other hand, those involved in the new thing are reluctant to give unqualified support to denominational churches lest they find themselves building up structures which they do not believe will survive the end-time shaking.

The antidote for protectiveness and exclusiveness is an overriding concern for the true unity and maturity of Christ's body. There must be a willingness for everything that the Heavenly

Father has not planted to be rooted up. Recovery always involves pulling down as well as building up. Without doubt, there will be costly adjustments, not simply in doctrine and practice, but also in spirit and attitude. But out of this, leaders will be brought out of independence into a committed relationship, which will result in great strength and security for the flock of God.

The prophetic Scriptures do not encourage us to believe that the final outpourings of the Spirit and the establishing of the Kingdom of God are to usher in a spiritual 'Utopia' before Christ returns. While the church is being brought to maturity, and the final great harvest is being gathered in, world conditions will continue to deteriorate. The trends we now see in society pointing towards its final disintegration will not be reversed by outpourings of the Spirit. Distress for the nations and tribulation for the church is predicted by the Spirit for the time of the end.

But the growing darkness will only make the light shining from God's people seem all the brighter. God will conclude this age as He commenced it. Great power and glory in the church, great victories over Satan, but in the context of great persecution and opposition. But the difference will be that what was then confined to one small corner of the globe will in the end be world-wide. I believe that the greatest chapters of the church's long history have yet to be written, and that it will be said of the generation that brings back the King, 'This was their finest hour.'

NOTES

1. Amos 3:7
2. Hab. 2:2
3. John 16:13
4. Eph. 1:11
5. Num. 23:19
6. Isa. 55:11
7. Joshua 23:14
8. Ps. 110:1-2
9. 1 Cor. 15:25
10. Heb. 10:12-13
11. Rom. 15:12-13 NIV
12. Acts 2:19-21
13. Eph. 4:4
14. John 17:20-23
15. Eph. 4:13 NASB